The Halex Family

Donated to

Mt. Norway YW

I
Walk
by
Faith

# I Walk by Faith

## ARDETH GREENE KAPP

Deseret Book Company
Salt Lake City, Utah

**Library of Congress Cataloging-in-Publication Data**

Kapp, Ardeth Greene, 1931–
    I walk by faith.

    Includes index.
    Summary: A collection of stories for young Mormon women illustrating the values of faith, divine nature, individual worth, knowledge, choice and accountability, good works, and integrity.
    1. Young women—Religious life.  [1. Christian life. 2. Conduct of life.  3. Mormons]  I. Title.
BX8656.K37   1987    248.4'89332033      87-5235
ISBN 0-87579-072-0

Printed in the United States of America

10   9   8   7   6   5

The following chapters are used by permission of The Church of Jesus Christ of Latter-day Saints: "All in One Family," "A Time for Hope," "Letters from Home," "My Dad Came After Me," "The Treasures We Take with Us," "Seek Learning by Study and Faith," "What Have You to Declare," and "Captains of Ten."

Lyrics used by permission of Janice Kapp Perry and Joy Lundberg: "The Rising Generation," "I Am of Infinite Worth," "I Walk by Faith," and "His Image in Your Countenance."

"Be That Friend," words and music by Michael H. McLean. ©1986 Shining Star Music (ASCAP). Used by permission.

# Contents

## Knowledge

## Choice and Accountability

## Good Works

## Integrity

# Preface

When we come to understand the purpose of this earth life, we develop increased determination, perseverance, optimism, and great faith. Our time here is a time of trial and testing to prepare us for all the blessings our Father in heaven has in store for us.

Away from our heavenly home, we occasionally have quiet longings for those things we once knew, the familiarity of our pre-earth life experiences, and our association with our Father in heaven in a family relationship. We were true and faithful there. And now a veil is drawn between our pre-earth life and our earth life, requiring us to walk by faith. We know that Satan and his influences are here to tempt us and persuade us to follow him as he endeavored to do there. We resisted; we stayed true to the teachings of our Father and his Son Jesus Christ then, and we are proving ourselves now.

We learn to walk by faith as we meet each day endeavoring to keep the commandments. Every law of God that we obey helps prepare us for our return home, our exaltation. Our Father in heaven has promised us that if we have faith in him and keep his commandments, we can always have his spirit to be with us, and one day we can return to his presence and dwell with him eternally. "God has reserved spirits for this dispensation, those who have the courage and the determination to face the world and all the powers of the evil one, visible and invisible, to proclaim the gospel and to maintain the truth and to establish and build up the

Zion of our God, fearless of all consequences." (George Q. Cannon, *Gospel Truth* 1:21-22.)

We are better able to walk by faith when we have an abiding assurance of who we really are, what our mission is, and what we are to accomplish in this time of testing away from our heavenly home. Our ultimate goal is to be true to our sacred covenants and to qualify for exaltation. In the song "I Walk By Faith," by Janice Kapp Perry, we learn of these things:

*I will prepare to make and keep sacred covenants,*
*Seek promised blessings of the priesthood through obedience,*
*Live my life to claim the blessing sweet of exaltation,*
*My testimony growing each new day.*
*I walk by faith, a daughter of heavenly parents.*
*Divine am I in nature by inheritance,*
*The Spirit whispers of my mission, my individual worth,*
*So I seek for precious knowledge, for learning and for growth.*

*I understand the meaning of accountability,*
*Every choice for good, for ill is my responsibility.*
*I want to build the kingdom, and good works is the key,*
*By doing what I know is right, I show integrity.*
*I walk by faith, a daughter of heavenly parents,*
*Divine am I in nature by inheritance,*
*And someday when God has proven me,*
*I will see him face to face,*
*But just for here and now, I walk by faith.*

As we learn to walk by faith, we witness miracles in our daily lives. "If there be no faith among the children of men God can do no miracles among them." (Ether 12:12.)

I am grateful for the thousands of young women who continually strengthen my faith as they walk by faith through happy and sometimes difficult times. The stories in this book are examples of valiant youths who have faced trials and tests, joys and successes, with growing and abiding faith. May these examples help you find joy in each day as you walk by faith—faith in the Lord Jesus Christ with assurance that "someday when God has proven me, I will see him face to face, but just for here and now, I walk by faith."

# Acknowledgments

I am grateful to my young friends in this rising generation whose inspiring examples bear evidence that they are taking their places and becoming a part of a mighty wave of righteous influence to the people in their own nations, as modern prophets and apostles have said they would. I am especially grateful to the young people who have allowed me to share their stories, although in some cases names have been changed in respect for their privacy.

I am thankful for my dear husband, Heber, whose constant support, encouragement, and faith in me give me courage to attempt projects like writing a book that I would otherwise never attempt.

A special thanks to my respected friend, Eleanor Knowles, who took the manuscript of my first book years ago and painstakingly edited, refined, and polished it, opening the door to my interest in writing. Today, some years later, she continues that skillful and painstaking task of editing, checking, and working through the transitions necessary for a polished manuscript.

And finally, I express thanks to the many friends I meet in my travels who express appreciation for my writings and give me courage to try again.

*Faith*

# All in One Family

Some years ago in the early spring, I took my little niece Shelly's hand in mine, and for hours we carefully picked our way from one rock to the next along a creek bed shaded by some tall trees. The gurgling water was like a musical accompaniment to the dance we were creating, as we would take a step, hesitate, reach, step forward, and then wait a moment to secure our balance.

Before long, we were drawn to an open meadow where some large cottonwood trees had been recently cut. Making my way through the tall grass, I held Shelly's hand as she climbed up on one fallen tree and, cautiously placing one foot ahead of the other, walked the full length of the tree and back again. We noticed tender green shoots forcing their way through the earth, and we saw the winter snow receding toward the mountain peaks. It seemed as though all of nature bore evidence of God's creations and his great love for us. Our afternoon activities continued until the evening breeze reminded us that our special day was coming to a close.

Approaching the narrow, steep garden path leading to my home, I let go of Shelly's hand, allowing her to go first. Our hands stuck together for a moment. A bond had formed from the warmth of the day through our shared adventures. Just before we reached the clearing near the house, I lifted Shelly up to see into a little nest built by a robin in the branch of a tree.

At the close of this memorable day, before tucking my niece (whom my sister shares with me) into bed, we knelt together while she expressed her thanks, which included gratitude for the creek, the slippery rocks, the big tree, and the robin's nest. Feeling a renewed appreciation for the same wonderful blessings, I tucked the covers around her and bent down for a good-night kiss. Reaching up, placing both arms around my neck, and pulling me close to her, Shelly whispered, "I wish we were in the same family."

"Shelly, my dear," I quickly explained, "we *are* in the same family."

"No, I mean the very same family. My last name is Larsen, and your last name is Kapp, and that isn't the same. I mean, I wish you were my sister and we had the very same last name."

Even though she was very young, I felt that she might sense security in our eternal relationship if I could somehow awaken within her a great eternal truth.

"Shelly, we really are in the very same family. You see, we are all our Heavenly Father's children, every one of us, and that makes us members of one great family. We are brothers and sisters, and Jesus is our brother, too, our elder brother."

"Then what is Jesus' last name?" she asked.

"Shelly, we know our Savior as Jesus the Christ." With the pure innocence of youth, she began to make us all one family by linking my first name with the surname "The Christ."

"Oh, no, my dear! We don't put our names together like that."

"But why not?" she asked.

Wanting her to be aware of the sacredness of our relationship with the Savior, I tried to explain: "I guess maybe it's because sometimes we are not good enough. I don't feel worthy yet."

With that, she raised up on her elbow. "What do you do that's wrong? Why don't you stop doing it, and then we can all be in the same family? We can all use his name."

I pondered the answer to her simple questions. I heard in my mind words as though I were hearing them for the first time. And yet, it had been only two days since I had attended sacrament meeting where I had listened to the same words. I had heard them with my ears so often before, but now it seemed different. It was as though I was hearing them with my whole heart and soul: "...that they are willing to take upon them the name of thy Son, and always remember him and keep his commandments which he has given them...." (D&C 20:77.)

Wasn't this the very thing we were talking about—the responsibility of taking upon ourselves that sacred name and committing to try always to remember him and keep his commandments?

While Shelly seemed secure and satisfied with the explanation given her at that time, over the years I have searched for deeper understanding of this sacred ordinance in which we renew our covenant each week to take upon ourselves Jesus' name. And while that usually occurs on Sunday, what does it mean on weekdays, and what difference does it make to a child, a youth, or an adult? Does it affect how we live our lives in the spring, summer, fall, or winter? Should it? Can we afford to consider this sacred ordinance passively and allow it to become routine in nature?

From the writings of C. S. Lewis we read, "Active habits are strengthened by repetition, but passive ones are weakened. The more often one feels without acting, the less he will be able ever to act, and, in the long run, the less he will be able to feel."

Jesus Christ came into the world "to be crucified for the world, and to bear the sins of the world, and to sanctify the world, and to cleanse it from all unrighteousness; that through him all might be saved." (D&C 76:41–42.)

There is no possible way we can ransom ourselves. It was Christ who suffered and died to atone for us. It was in the Garden of Gethsemane that his sufferings were beyond all mortal comprehension, that the weight of our sins caused him to feel such agony, pain, and heartbreak that he bled from every pore, suffering in both body and spirit. When we see in our minds by the gift of the Spirit the reality of Gethsemane, it is his great love for us that gives us the strength to struggle and suffer in our small way to overcome our sins. Can we possibly comprehend such love? It is this atonement that can, if we will just do our part, ransom us, qualify us, redeem us, save us, and exalt us.

Our part, then, is to accept Christ's atonement by repenting of our sins, being baptized, receiving the Holy Ghost, and obeying all the commandments. When we became members of his church at the time of baptism, we covenanted with him to take upon ourselves his name. Do we remember that baptismal covenant every day and do what we really want to do in relation to that important event in our lives?

Not long ago at the closing session of a youth conference, just as the young priest conducting the meeting stood to bring the meeting to a close, Kathy, sitting next to me, jumped up, slipped in front of the young man, and took her place at the pulpit. Facing the audience, she raised both hands with outstretched fingers and said, "I'll bet you've all been wondering why I've been wearing this ugly green nail polish." A soft ripple could be heard across the audience, and I realized I was not alone in my curiosity.

"Well," she said, "it's like this: I knew my responsibilities as one of the leaders of this conference were big. I knew I had some real challenges ahead, and I didn't want to be sorry after the chance was gone that I didn't do what I really wanted to do. I needed something that would remind me of what I really wanted to do and help me through the things I didn't want to do. So I thought of a plan. And it worked! You see," she went on, "I wanted something that would remind me of what I really wanted to make myself do. I knew my fingernails would always be right there."

After further details, and bearing a strong testimony of the joy that comes when you do what you should, she took her seat. From this insight I was reminded of the message of the Apostle Paul as he was counseling the Corinthians: "When I was a child, I spake as a child, I understood as a child, I thought as a child: but when I became a man, I put away childish things." (1 Corinthians 13:11.)

Kathy had helped us all understand the importance of reminders, but it was the combined voices of young people singing the closing song, resounding like a sacred sermon, that brought forth new appreciation for sacred reminders. They sang:

> *I marvel that he would descend from his throne divine*
> *To rescue a soul so rebellious and proud as mine;*
> *That he should extend his great love unto such as I,*
> *Sufficient to own, to redeem, and to justify.*

You and I and Shelly, all of us, have the sacrament, a holy priesthood ordinance that helps remind us of the atonement of the Savior. It helps us keep focused on our daily progress toward exaltation. It is a precious and sacred reminder, not just on Sunday, but on Monday, Tuesday, and Wednesday; spring, summer, and fall; when we're on the mountain peaks of our lives and also in the valleys. What is true for Shelly and you and me is that our Savior loves us very much.

Speaking of the Son of God, we read in Alma 7:11–13: "And he shall go forth, suffering pains and afflictions and temptations of every kind; and this that the word might be fulfilled which saith he will take upon him the pains and the sicknesses of his people. And he will take upon him . . . their infirmities, that his bowels may be filled with mercy, according to the flesh, that he may know according to the flesh how to succor his people according to their infirmities."

President Marion G. Romney's insight has made a change in my life regarding the opportunity that is mine to partake of the sacrament. He said: "Now partaking of the sacrament is not to be a mere passive experience. We are *not* to remember the Lord's suffering and death only as we may remember some purely secular historical event. Participating in the sacrament service is meant to be a vital and a spiritualizing experience. Speaking of it, the Savior said: '. . . and it shall be a testimony unto the Father that ye do always remember me.' (3 Nephi 18:4–9.)

"In order to testify, one's mind has to function, and it must be concentrated upon the thing to be testified. And we are not only to partake of the emblems of the sacrament in remembrance of the Redeemer, testifying that we do always remember him, but we are also thereby to witness unto the Father that we are willing to take upon us the name of his Son and that we *will* keep his commandments. Now there is a doctrine abroad in the world today which teaches that the physical emblems of the sacrament are transformed into the flesh and blood of Jesus. We do not teach such doctrine, for we know that any transformation which comes from the administration of the sacrament takes place in the souls of those who understandingly partake of it. It is the participating individuals who are affected and they are affected in a most marvelous way, for they are given the Spirit of the Lord to be with them." (*Conference Report,* April 1946, p. 47.)

At those very times when we feel least worthy, least comfortable about carrying his holy name, and have a keener sense of our imperfections, those moments when the flesh is weak and our spirits suffer disappointment knowing what we *can* become, we might feel a sense of withdrawing, a pulling away, a feeling of needing to set aside for a time at least that divine relationship with the Savior until we are more worthy. It is at that very moment, even in our unworthiness, that the offer is again given to us to accept the great gift of the atonement—even before we change. When you feel the need to pull away, will you reach out to him? Instead of feeling the need to resist, will you submit to his will?

It is in our struggles, while striving to qualify, that our spirit reaches out in greater humility and gratitude, and we are better prepared to receive the gift because we so desperately need it—in fact, we *must* have it if we are to receive any eternal rewards.

At the time my father was in the last stages of stomach cancer, his body wasting away to less than one hundred pounds, his spirit growing in strength every single day, he shared with me his new insights from that perspective. It is a fact, he bore witness, that the body and the spirit are separate. When this process of separation is witnessed firsthand, he said with conviction and enthusiasm, the meaning of eternal life and the resurrection takes on a new dimension of understanding. It is like discovering a precious gift you've held in your possession all this time but never unwrapped: when the time comes to open it, you're more ready to appreciate the divine nature of the gift because you are prepared to use it for the purpose for which it was intended.

The purpose of the sacramental covenant is always in force. I would now say to Shelly, "Yes, my dear, put my name with the Savior's." He said we could. He wants us to. He wants us to feel comfortable carrying his name. And when we feel the greatest need, that divine gift can penetrate our souls and we can open it and use it for what it was intended.

We must come to the sacrament altar hungry, with a spiritual hunger and thirst for righteousness. It is a time for self-evaluation, a time to rectify our course, if necessary, a time to decide to make right everything in our lives. It is a time and place for us to judge ourselves, to come to understand better the magnitude of being allowed to have his Spirit with us always to direct every act of our lives.

I believe that each new day can be faced with greater anticipation and purpose when we are reminded of the words of Elder John A. Widtsoe: "There is a spiritual meaning of all human acts and earthly events. No man is quite so happy, I think, as he who backs all his labors by . . . a spiritual interpretation and understanding of the acts of life. A piece of silver always has a certain value as it passes from hand to hand; it is weighed and we sell it in the marketplace; but, when that piece of silver is coined into a dollar, it receives the stamp of government service; it becomes a coin of the realm, and it moves from hand to hand to accomplish the work of the realm. So, every act of man, the moment it is fitted into the great plan, the plan of salvation, receives spiritual coinage, and passes from hand to hand, from mind to mind, to accomplish the greater work of God." ( *Conference Report,* April 1922, pp. 96-97.)

As we gradually move to that spiritual level, we will begin to experience that partnership to which we agreed in our premortal existence—to help to bring salvation and eternal life to everyone under the plan.

When the Spirit becomes our constant companion, each day will be different, and with the Spirit reflected in our language, in our daily work, at school, on the street, and in the marketplace, slowly, day by day, our conduct will become more unselfish, our relationships more tender, our desire to serve more constant, and we will find ourselves going about doing good. Always. We will have taken upon us not only His name but also His image in our countenances. (See Alma 5:14.)

This experiment has been tried before, even in Christ's lifetime. A few men were admitted to the inner circle of his friendship, and, day by day, these first disciples began to mellow and soften and grow spiritually with power and strength and influence. For Paul, the process was more dramatic. On the road to Damascus he met the Savior, and from that time his words, his deeds, his career, his daily walk were different.

Have we experienced this encounter on our Damascus road or maybe in a less dramatic way? When this happens, we will be allowed to witness miracles. We will better understand them and even participate in them. Lives will be changed when we begin to see each other as our Savior sees us. We will want to teach each other the way he would teach us. We will yearn for the spirituality to bear testimony to each other of the things to which he bears testimony. And when we meet, it will be as someone said: "We will not just exchange words; what we will exchange is souls." Not just with our friends and loved ones, but with all for whom we share a responsibility for their eternal welfare. With the Spirit we will be allowed to see things not as the world sees them but more as Jesus would see them. We will learn to hearken to the voice of the Spirit.

President Romney, speaking to a group of sisters who were being released from a calling in the Church, said in part, "I pray that the Lord will help you to live every day so you can have the Spirit of the Lord with you. It is a wonderful thing to try to know and to try to live so that you can hear and respond to the voice of the Lord. That's where the comfort comes in this life. . . . Hearken to the voice of the Spirit and have the discernment to know what the Spirit tells you. Then have the courage to follow that counsel."

One day I witnessed evidence of the Spirit and the courage to follow counsel. It was in a second grade elementary classroom. The student teacher held the children captive with her storytelling skills. In great detail she told of a cross old man whose name was Mr. Black. In contrast, the account was given in similar detail of a Mr. Brown who was kind and thoughtful and loved by everyone. At the conclusion of the story, the teacher asked the children, "How many of you would like to be a neighbor to Mr. Brown?" Every hand was raised high. Then, almost as an afterthought, she inquired if there was anyone who would like to have Mr. Black for a neighbor.

A little boy in a faded green shirt near the back of the room began to raise his hand, which brought a ripple of quiet amusement from the children. Hesitating only briefly, he looked around at his friends and still mustered the courage to hold his hand high and to stand alone in his difference. When called on for an explanation to his single vote, he spoke in a soft tone. "Well," he said, "I'd like Mr. Black to be my neighbor, because if he was, my mom would make a cake for me to take to him, and then he wouldn't be that way anymore." A hush fell over the room. Everyone felt something wonderful that they couldn't explain. A little child broke the silence like a benediction: "Oh, I wish I'd said that!"

We had all made a quick decision about who would be the best neighbor, but only one, just one, had a spirit within, a discernment, that allowed him to see what might be.

Another day I witnessed the need for the Spirit to help guide the service that was being performed by well-meaning neighbors. A widow said to me, "I don't need more food. My freezer is literally full of the neighbors' cakes and pies and goodies. But I need someone to invite me to go to Temple Square with them and their children to see the Christmas lights. You don't really see the lights without the children." Sometimes it's cake, but sometimes it isn't. The Spirit will help us customize our service.

President Spencer W. Kimball said, "God does notice us, and he watches over us. But it is usually through another person that he meets our needs." (*Ensign,* December 1974, p. 5.) I believe it is one who hears when the Lord is calling.

Consider now, even at this moment, the brother or sister next to you, or one nearby, through the hall, across the street, or down the road. Will you put yourself so in tune that you can try to see in that person what the Savior sees? Will you share with that brother or sister something that would ease their load or brighten their day, or expand their vision, or increase their hope, and try to do it the way you think the Savior might do it? Could you? Would you?

Given the opportunities available to each of us this very week to live the sacramental life, can you feel within you a growing strength, a yearning desire, an increased commitment to reach out? Will you consider seriously what truth of which you have a personal witness that you could teach another, and teach it in partnership with the Savior, even to the person sitting next to you who might be a stranger though a brother or sister?

If you will sincerely try to do this, something sweet and gentle will surround you. Voices will be softened, hearts will be touched, a deep feeling of caring will swell up within, and you will feel the Spirit, even as you serve in Jesus' name. It will be a spiritual experience, the kind each of us yearns for and can have when we remember him and have his Spirit with us. It is in reaching out to others that we qualify ourselves and become more worthy of his name. It is our ordinary work, our seemingly routine duties, and our familiar relationships that can become sacramental in nature.

One day I witnessed that great joy while sitting beside a friend. He had recently been called as a mission president, and I thought, "What could I share with him at this important time in his life?" I endeavored to see in him what I thought the Lord might see in him. I desired to say something that would be of importance to him at this time. I had a wonderful feeling of love for my longtime friend and felt prompted to share the thoughts that came into my mind.

"I guess at a time like this," I said to him, "one feels an increased urgency to be a pure vessel through which the Spirit can work unrestrained. Yet isn't it marvelous to know that you will have access to that great power, that inspiration, and even revelation every day while you and your missionaries are still striving for perfection?"

Almost immediately his eyes were moist. His chin quivered and he said, "You must have known I needed to hear that."

When we are in the church, on the bus, in the grocery store, in the classroom, and most important, in our homes, let us strive to see each other the way we think Jesus might; and, sensing each other's divine potential, let us take the opportunity to share an eternal truth that will be personalized because the Spirit prompts us. In the closing moments of the Savior's life, while he suffered for us, he told us how we can be his disciples: "A new commandment I give unto you, That ye love one another; as I have loved you, that ye also love one another. By this shall all men know that ye are my disciples, if ye have love one to another." (John 13:34-35.)

Every act of our lives *can* become a sacramental experience when we take upon us his name. Then, when our performance falls short in spite of our striving for perfection, we will find ourselves eagerly and anxiously, and with a deeper sense of gratitude than ever before, drawn to the Sabbath day and the sacramental altar. There we can feel the glorious transformation and healing of our wounded spirits as we commit to strive again and again to follow him. With a new day and a new week and a new opportunity we will welcome another chance to feel more deeply, to care more sincerely, to understand more compassionately, to teach more purposefully, to remember him always, and to have his Spirit to be with us.

As I held Shelly's little hand in mine for one last squeeze before tiptoeing from her room that evening some years ago, a feeling of gratitude and reverence came flooding forth. I realized that while her hand had been in mine for most of the afternoon as I helped her through the creek, across the rocks, and over the tree and lifted her up to see the miracle of life unfolding in a robin's nest, this child had led me to begin a search that would lead me to a better understanding of a great eternal truth. King Benjamin explained it for us: "And now, because of the covenant which ye have made ye shall be called the children of Christ, his sons, and his daughters; for behold, this day he hath spiritually begotten you; for ye say that your hearts are changed through faith on his name; therefore, ye are born of him and have become his sons and his daughters." (Mosiah 5:7.)

We can all be members of the same family. If you're doing something you shouldn't, consider Shelly's question to me: Why don't you stop? It may not always be easy, but with his help you can overcome.

# My Prayer Was Answered

On board the British Airways flight that morning, we waited for the jet to pull away from the gate. We were parked at the gate at Heathrow Airport in London, on a flight that would arrive in Oslo, Norway, within little more than an hour. This would make the seventh country we had visited within the past twenty-one days. Just four more countries, seven more days, and we would be boarding a plane in Helsinki, Finland, for a brief stop in Copenhagen, Denmark, and then home. Getting on and off planes each day for a month had become almost as routine as getting up, brushing our teeth, combing our hair, eating breakfast, and going to work.

My husband and I had been traveling with one small piece of luggage apiece that, with just a little juggling, would fit under the seat in front of us. In addition to these two small pieces containing our clothes and a few personal belongings (much less than you would ever think you could get along with at home), we had taken one lightweight tan canvas bag I had borrowed from a friend. In this bag was everything we couldn't possibly get along without, except our passports and money, which we carried in our jackets in a special folder accessible at all times. In the canvas bag were the complete records of our trip so far: names and addresses, records of meetings held, all the details needed to prepare the reports that would be expected upon our return home. In one pocket of the bag was a small tape recorder with several tapes on which I had dictated many letters and instructions as a follow-up to commitments I had made to people in six countries. In addition, there were two small cameras with about eight rolls of film used to record the memories of places visited and people we had met, and my small set of scriptures, which had finally become as familiar to me as the old set that I had reluctantly given up for the advantage of the additional references in the new edition.

While all of these things were of great importance, even more essential were the transparencies in Norwegian, Swedish, Finnish, and Danish that I desperately needed for the training I had come so far to do. With these visual aids, which had been translated to facilitate the difficulty of language barriers, I had discovered that little was lost in the process of communication.

The plane was about to pull away from the gate, so we fastened our seat belts as instructed. By now we felt like seasoned travelers. The only thing different about this part of the journey was that instead of carrying our small suitcases on the plane to place under the seat in front of us, for the first time we had been asked to check them through to Oslo when we went through the security check. We were somewhat relieved to be free of luggage for the first time. It felt different, like releasing your arm from a sling after it finally healed. With nothing to do now but sit back and relax until we reached our next destination, Heber turned to me and asked, "Where did you put the tan bag?" "The bag?" I sat up straight and the seatbelt pulled tight across my legs. "Don't you have it?" I asked. "I thought you had it," he said. Suddenly he released his seat belt and began to get out of his seat. The tan canvas bag was missing—the one we did not need to check through. We were to carry it with us. With the change of routine and the unexpected freedom from carrying our bags, neither of us had picked up the case with all our records!

Heber quickly made his way to the front of the plane. The aisles were clear, with the passengers all buckled in their seats for take-off. He left the plane, and I waited in my seat for only a moment, then followed him to the door. The flight attendants were ready to close the door of this giant jet with me on the inside and Heber on the outside—and that arrangement simply was not acceptable. I stood at the door as if to stop the plane from taking off without him and explained that my husband had left the plane. The steward threw up his hands and said, "Lady, we can't hold up this plane. You will have to either get off or take your seat." "Just one minute," I pleaded. "Just one minute."

I left the plane and ran the short distance to the building, where Heber and an airport employee stood in serious conversation. Heber turned to me. "It isn't here," he said. "What shall we do?" A decision had to be made fast; there was no time to consider many alternatives. We could both stay and go back through the different areas where we had been waiting during the past ninety minutes and hope to retrieve our missing luggage, but what about the people who would be waiting to meet us in Oslo? And what about those who were gathering for the meeting that was to be held within an hour after our arrival? Surely that was not the right alternative. There was another possibility. I could go on and Heber could remain behind to look for the luggage and then come on a later flight. The insecurity that accompanies traveling without being able to speak the language, meeting people you've never met before, and the uncertainty of a later flight all added up to one decision. We must board the plane immediately and take our assigned seats.

The airport attendant understood our plight and agreed to see what he could do to track our missing luggage while we were in flight. We were mindful that during the past hour and a half a voice had droned over the loudspeaker, "Do not leave any luggage unattended." I had paid little attention to the instruction. We already knew we should not leave our luggage unattended. After we had been checked through security, we had been directed from one waiting room to another three different times. The burning question "Where did we leave the bag?" was less important than the anxiety caused by the question "Will we ever get it back?" and of greater concern was "How?" The attendant assured us he would see what he could do, and if the bag could be located, he would try to get it on the next flight to Oslo, Norway.

With only a glimmer of hope and a knot in my stomach, I took Heber's arm and we returned to the plane, where we met impatient looks in the eyes of our fellow travelers. I wanted to stand up and explain it all so they could share in our anxiety, but I realized we carried our burden alone. We sank into our seats and fastened our seat belts. There wasn't much to say. In fact, it had all been said. Talking at this point would do little good. We both looked out of the window as we taxied down the runway and lifted into the air, leaving the enormous Heathrow Airport, where masses of humanity move through daily to link up with all parts of the world.

High in the air, far above the clouds, is a good place to consider what resources might be called upon to save the day. I closed my eyes and began praying. While I could not appropriately get in a kneeling position, it made little difference to the intensity of my prayer. Each morning and each night before retiring we had reported in. We had expressed thanks for protection in our travels and had asked that we be able to make all of our connections and maintain the necessary health and strength to accomplish the purpose of our mission. After three weeks with every detail working so smoothly, it is easy to become casual about blessings given that are hardly realized. But this time there was nothing casual about my prayer. We needed help! What if the bag could not be located? What if it was located but the tapes, the records, the transparencies, or any other item had been taken? What if I had to conduct the long training meetings for which people had traveled such long distances and had no materials in their language and not even scriptures in my own? What would I ever do? I had never been very good at finding my favorite scriptures in someone else's books, and I knew for sure that I couldn't do so in Norwegian, Finnish, Danish, or Swedish.

With my eyes closed from the time we left London until the flight attendant interrupted my thoughts with instructions to fasten our seat belts and return our trays to the locked position for landing in Oslo, I prayed fervently. Into my mind came comforting words that I had marked in my scriptures that were now somewhere far away. In my mind, as if on a page in front of me, I read: "Wherefore, as ye are agents, ye are on the Lord's errand; and whatever ye do according to the will of the Lord is the Lord's business." (D&C 64:29.) Surely I am on the Lord's business, I consoled myself. There had been little or no time for anything else. My mind jumped from the Doctrine and Covenants to the Book of Mormon. I had read and even memorized the statement of Nephi about how he trusted in the Lord, but this time the words had even greater meaning. "I will go and do the things which the Lord hath commanded, for I know that the Lord giveth no commandments unto the children of men, save he shall prepare a way for them that they may accomplish the thing which he hath commanded them." (1 Nephi 3:7.) If I was to accomplish the thing I had been asked to do, I felt that I must have that bag. The question was, how would it be returned to me?

Could an angel be dispatched, if necessary, to watch over that bag and get it from England to Norway? I wondered. I opened my mental scriptures again to the book of Ether, to that great chapter on faith where Moroni says, "Ye receive not witness until after the trial of your faith." And then came the statement, "For if there be no faith among the children of men God can do no miracle among them." (Ether 12:12.)

By now a calm, warm feeling was forming in my heart, interrupted by the thought, But what if the bag doesn't show up? I began to remember all the seemingly less important prayers that I knew had been answered in the past and thought that if those were answered, surely this prayer would be heard and answered. Again that warm feeling returned. In my mind I could see my friends, members of the Young Women general board, praying for me at home as we always did each Wednesday night for any of our number who were away on assignments. I remembered a drawer full of letters in my desk from young women all over the world saying that they were praying for me. Finally, I could see in my mind's eye the homes of my sisters, with their families gathered around their breakfast tables in the morning and in their living rooms in the evening, kneeling in prayer. I knew we would be included in those prayers. In answer to my own fervent prayer mingled with theirs, a warm feeling enveloped me from my head to my toes.

With the assurance that the bag would be returned, I turned my attention to the challenge I would face at the first meeting that afternoon, before the late-afternoon flight arrived from England. I put my concern for the evening meeting and the subsequent meetings out of my mind for a time. It was that one o'clock meeting that I must give attention to right now.

Again I considered what scripture I would like to read if only I had my scriptures. I again turned the pages in my mind and read from the Doctrine and Covenants: "Neither take ye thought beforehand what ye shall say; but treasure up in your minds continually the words of life, and it shall be given you in the very hour that portion that shall be meted unto every man." (D&C 84:85.) And how will this happen, I thought, without my outlines and my scriptures?

The promises of the Lord came to my mind: "I will go before your face. I will be on your right hand and on your left, and my Spirit shall be in your hearts, and mine angels round about you, to bear you up." (D&C 84:88.)

As the plane landed, Heber broke the silence. "Everything is going to be all right," he assured me.

We waited our turn to leave the plane, full of anticipation at meeting strangers who in an instant would be our brothers and sisters and shortly thereafter would seem like dear and long-time friends. At the bottom of the stairs, a representative of British Airways stopped us, asked our name, and advised us that he had received a telex with the news that our bag had been located and would arrive on the six o'clock flight that evening. He told us where we might pick it up at that time. With thanks more grateful than he could possibly have realized, we expressed our deep appreciation.

As we turned to leave, Heber noticed a shiny coin on the concrete near his foot. He picked it up, recognized it as a foreign coin of a small denomination, and handed it to me, saying, "Let this be your faith coin, a reminder of this experience." I tucked the coin in my pocket, and we proceeded to look for the people who were meeting us. We did not tell them of our experience lest we raise any concern about our preparation for the meeting.

At the conclusion of the afternoon meeting, the stake president stood before the audience and expressed appreciation for "some of the finest training we have ever had." The words of Ammon in the Book of Mormon came flooding to my mind: "I do not boast in my own strength, nor in my own wisdom; but behold, my joy is full, yea, my heart is brim with joy, and I will rejoice in my God. Yea, I know that I am nothing; as to my strength I am weak; therefore I will not boast of myself, but I will boast of my God, for in his strength I can do all things; yea, behold, many mighty miracles we have wrought in this land, for which we will praise his name forever." (Alma 26:11–12.)

Before the seven o'clock meeting, the tan canvas bag that belonged to my friend and contained all that I needed to fill my assignment was in my hands, not a thing missing.

Sometimes when I feel concern for things beyond my ability to solve, I find myself fingering my little faith coin, and that familiar warm feeling starts in the region of my heart, and I remember.

*Faith*

# A Time for Hope

I wish I could sit with you in the swing on my back porch, just as the sun is going down. It is so fun to listen to the crickets. Those who have trained themselves to listen well can distinguish between a cricket's love call, a danger signal, and other messages that simply say "I'm here." Did you know that crickets actually listen with ears that are located on their knees? When I'm on my knees I try to listen—listen that I might better understand the needs, the wants, the yearnings of the young women of the Church. I do this when I read their letters and whenever I have an opportunity to hear them speak their thoughts and feelings.

Imagine yourself sitting with me in the swing on my back porch, and together we will listen to the messages in some letters I have received from young women recently.

> Dear Sister Kapp: This year I have had a hard time with my
> *self-esteem* and with my friend (who is also LDS) turning
> on me and going off with other friends. Sometimes I feel
> terribly lonely. I know Heavenly Father is aware of my
> problems but I also know that I must have them to grow,
> even though that is hard to remember sometimes.

Let us listen to another young woman who pours out the feelings of her heart:

They always say something must happen in your life so
you want to change. Well, that something has happened. I
still have a long way to go. I finally realized that my Father
in heaven is on my side even though I have betrayed him
in a way. I am trying awfully hard to get my life in order
and do what is right. I am bound and determined to do so,
no matter how long it takes, but it is so hard. I just wish I
could go up and give Heavenly Father and Heavenly
Mother a big hug and tell them that I made it back.

Let us listen to part of a letter received by an anxious but grateful
mother. Her seventeen-year-old daughter, who would be considered a troublemaker by some who have not learned to recognize
her call for help, writes:

Dear Mom and Dad: I know I haven't been much of a
daughter. I really hope things can get better between us.
Please don't give up on me. Just because I don't say I love
you doesn't mean I don't. Please understand what I am trying to say. We'll stay together and love each other through
the worst and hardest times. We'll make it 'cause we're a
family.

I hear these messages from our precious young women. I hear
them with my ears and my heart. I want to reach out to each one and
share with her what I have learned over the years about hope. I
would give hope to you too, if I could, yet I have learned that hope
comes only from our own upward climb. You see, this brief time
away from our heavenly home and parents is a time when we are
given our agency for the purpose of being tried and tested in every
way. (See 2 Nephi 2:24–28.) We can expect some down days and
some hard tests. But if we learn from them and grow from them, we
will each be stronger and better because of them. Whenever I face
things that are difficult and that I don't understand, I repeat in my
mind the words of a song I learned years ago when I wondered if my
prayers were being heard and I needed hope to carry on:

*In the furnace God may prove thee,*
*Thence to bring thee forth more bright,*

*But can never cease to love thee;*
*Thou art precious in his sight.*
*God is with thee, God is with thee;*
*Thou shalt triumph in his might.*

My sister Sharon had a record that she played over and over until she memorized the lines, and she still repeats them to me on occasion. It tells the story of a young girl in a small mining town in Leadville, Colorado. She was found by some backwoods people. They didn't know where she came from, but they took her in and raised her. She had a drive and a hope inside her that took her in time from that tiny mining town in Colorado to some of the most prestigious places in all of Europe.

As the musical version of Molly Brown's story unfolds, we see her first as a young, backwoods girl with few opportunities, no education, and no refinement. She is wrestling with her adopted brothers, who get her down. Her brother says, "You're down, Molly. You're down." And young Molly responds, "I ain't down. I ain't down. And even if I was, you'd sure never hear it from me. I hate the word *down* but I love the word *up,* 'cuz up means hope, and that's just what I got. Hope for someplace prettier, someplace cleaner. And if I've gotta eat catfish heads all my life, can't I eat them off a plate just once and in a red silk dress?" Then she begins to sing at the top of her lungs. "And then someday, with all my might and my main, I'm gonna learn to read and write. I'm gonna see what there is to see. And if you're goin' from nowhere on the road to somewhere and you meet anyone, you'll know it's me." Does that sound like hope to you?

Molly's hope and determination took her to great heights. Then one day she found herself on the ill-fated *Titanic,* which sank to the bottom of the ocean with more than a thousand people on board. But Molly Brown did not go down. She managed to get into one of the lifeboats with a few others, and she began rowing. It was dark and cold, and the survivors were gripped with the fear of a watery grave. Some cried out in anguish, "We can't make it!" But Molly refused to give up. She just kept rowing. The headlines of the *New York Times* called her "the unsinkable Molly Brown." She was full of hope, and her unwavering hope inspired others with hope.

I used to wonder about that road to somewhere that Molly sang about, and how I'd ever find it. As a young girl I remember standing at the kitchen window of our home and looking down the gravel road toward the east as far as I could see. On each side of the road was tall grass in the summer and deep snow in the winter, and there were only a few houses sprinkled along the way. I used to wonder, "What is out there for me? Where do I belong?" I'm sure you must wonder that sometimes. Things didn't seem too hopeful at that time. School had been very difficult for me. My friends were moving on without me, and I felt dumb. Do you have any idea what that feels like? It's awful.

When I was twelve years old and feeling very discouraged after a long, hard winter, my mom and dad had a plan they worked out at some sacrifice that they hoped would give me hope. They determined to take me with them beyond our gravel road, out across the Canadian border, through the big states of Montana and Idaho, and on to Salt Lake City, Utah, the headquarters of the Church, to attend general conference.

We arrived early on the first day of conference and waited in line, hoping to enter the great dome-shaped Tabernacle, which I had seen only in pictures. Finally we found seats in the balcony, where I could look down and actually see the prophet in real life, and hear him speak, a thing I had never dreamed would ever happen to me. The feeling I had at that time was one of hope, and I began to understand about the real road to somewhere. I determined right then to plant my feet on that road, the straight and narrow path leading to the celestial kingdom, and to never ever give up. I have come to know without any question that the gospel of Jesus Christ is the pathway to hope that leads us back to our Heavenly Father and our eternal home.

Listen to our Father's promise to us. He says, "Be faithful and diligent in keeping the commandments of God, and I will encircle thee in the arms of my love." (D&C 6:20.) And he comforts us, saying, "Come unto me, all ye that labour and are heavy laden, and I will give you rest. Take my yoke upon you, and learn of me; for I am meek and lowly in heart: and ye shall find rest unto your souls." (Matthew 11:28-29.)

Now if we were sitting together on my back porch, I would stop and ask you, "Do you understand the plan of our Heavenly Father and your part in it?" To every young woman, I plead: Find your own back porch, away from the demanding, loud voices of the world. Learn to listen, not to the crickets, but to the constant whisperings of the Spirit with its messages of hope that will prompt you each step of the way on your road to the celestial kingdom.

Can you imagine what could happen if every young woman were to send out a message of hope to the world that would inspire others to never give up? That is exactly what has happened. All 300,000 young women of the Church were invited recently to participate in a magnificent, worldwide celebration. They were invited to prepare brief messages of love and hope to the world and attach them to helium-filled balloons that were released at sunrise on a memorable fall day.

Angela Santana sent her message of love from Brazil: "Peace is what we feel when we live righteously. It is having the Spirit with us who testifies about our Heavenly Father and his Son, Jesus Christ. It is preparing for the day when we can live in the kingdom of heaven with our Heavenly Father eternally." On the envelope she printed, "If a man still has hope, he is never completely unhappy."

Shauna Bocutt, age fifteen, from Kinshasa, Zaire, in Africa, sent her message of hope and included this personal testimony: "I know my Heavenly Father loves me because I have asked."

From the Philippines, Dhezie Jimeno wrote: "I would like to share with you a message which I hope you'll keep to your heart's delight. The message is that God cares and loves you very, very much. Yes, in life we experience pain and heartaches, sorrows and tribulations, but mind you, all these things are just to give us experience, and besides, we can make them work for our own good. Difficulties are just God's errand. If we are sent upon them, it is an evidence of his confidence. Therefore, let us be glad, be happy, for it is a way of being wise. God loves you, and he is ever willing to help you at all times. Just call on him through fervent prayers. I know God never fails; he is there, he is listening, and he cares very deeply about you. You've got a friend."

With the gospel in our lives and our feet firmly planted on the road to the celestial kingdom, we can move forward and upward. There will be some steep climbs ahead, but our Lord and Savior

Jesus Christ has covenanted and promised to climb with us every step of the way. Your hope, when united with the hope of thousands of others, can bring the light and the hope of the gospel of Jesus Christ to a troubled world. Covenant this very day (if you haven't already) to plant your feet firmly on the path to the celestial kingdom, and never ever give up. This time, above all other times, is a time for hope.

*Faith*

# Letters from Home

How I wish I could sit on the edge of your bed with you, look into your eyes, and feel the greatness of your spirit. We'd talk about the desire to be popular and the influence of peers and the importance of families and the good times. You would tell me about when you have felt discouraged, disappointed, confused, or afraid.

I think of questions young women have asked me. "How do I stay close to the Lord?" "Can I make it?" "Is there a way back?" In answer to those questions, I raise my voice and say with all the fervor of my soul, "You can feel a closeness to your Heavenly Father. You can make it no matter how tough the test." And to some I'd say with the deepest conviction, "Yes, there is a way. Come back."

I would tell you how studying the scriptures can make it easier to know all the things Heavenly Father wants us to do. I remember a difficult time in my life when I thought I couldn't make it. I had failed a grade in school. I was humiliated and lacked confidence in myself and my abilities. It was awful. I didn't want to go on. I remember praying with all my heart that I could be smart. Sometime after that, I became aware that the scriptures could help me find answers when I needed help. I'd like to share with you one scripture that really helped me at that time in my life: "Trust in the Lord with all thine heart; and lean not unto thine own understanding. In all thy ways acknowledge him, and he shall direct thy paths." (Proverbs 3:5–6.)

You might think that I never lack confidence now, but I do

sometimes. And when I feel that way, I reread that scripture. I can feel his love and the secure, quiet feeling of peace, and know he is near.

You might wonder how this happens. Maybe you're like many young people—you find the scriptures boring, or they don't have much meaning to you. Learning to love the scriptures is a lot like learning to walk. At first you're unsure—you sometimes stumble, and you don't get anywhere very fast. If you stopped trying to walk just because you fell down a few times, you'd never know the joy of walking. But once you learn how to walk, soon you can run and go places you couldn't go before.

Let me tell you how learning to walk is like learning to study the scriptures. When you first begin reading the scriptures, you feel unsure; you'd much rather read something familiar, like a favorite story. But I can tell you from experience that if you will try reading the scriptures every day, just as you kept trying to walk, the scriptures will be as important to you as being able to walk. In fact, I believe they will be more important. But you've got to begin. If you haven't done so already, start tonight by marking a favorite scripture before you go to bed. Just take a step or two each day. If you don't have a favorite scripture, you could mark the one I shared from Proverbs and put today's date beside it.

You might start by first reading the chapter headings to get the sense of the story. I'd suggest that you start with Third Nephi in the Book of Mormon. The heading of chapter one reads, in part, "The night of Christ's birth arrives—the sign is given and a new star arises." You're already familiar with that miraculous story, and by reading this chapter, you can be comfortably on your way—a first step that can lead to many more each day.

Recently I spent three days in a wilderness camp with 150 young people. We did a lot of hiking and had some hard physical challenges, such as rappelling down an eighty-foot cliff. On the last day we were given instructions to go into the woods alone. Before leaving the group, each youth was given a letter from home that had been written by one of his or her parents for this occasion.

When I went out alone, I took my scriptures with me. I read about the love of our Father in heaven for all of us and for me. And right then I realized that the scriptures are like letters from home.

After the time alone, we gathered together to share our experiences. Many spoke of their letter from home. One young woman stood before us and expressed the feelings of her heart as she held her letter from home close—a precious treasure. She told us, "I bawled my face off when I sat there alone and realized how much my mom and dad love me."

It can be that same way for each of us when we read the scriptures. Can you imagine being away from home and receiving a letter from your parents and not bothering to open and read it? This is what happens when we don't read the scriptures. The scriptures are like letters from home telling us how much our Heavenly Father loves us. They tell us how we can draw near to him. He tells us to come as we are; no one will be denied. (See 3 Nephi 9:14, 17–18.)

Open your scriptures and read them every day. Why? So you can have a sure testimony of his love for you. So you can know the gospel plan and the blessings that come through obedience and right choices. So you will have many, many scriptures marked that you can turn to quickly for comfort, for courage, for faith and hope and peace, and for wisdom and joy, and experience the feelings of being close to him. The verses you mark will become anchors to cling to when the voices of the world confuse you. They will lift you up in spirit and literally save your life when you're down. If you will ask Heavenly Father in your daily prayers to help you understand the messages, and if you will strive to keep the commandments, you can have the spirit of the Holy Ghost to teach you and to open your mind to the special messages that are there for you for your needs at particular times in your life.

I know this is true. It can happen over and over again. It has happened for me. Often, while you're studying, you will feel very close to your Heavenly Father, and you will want to have your scriptures with you always to renew that feeling over and over again.

I have a set of scriptures in a small size so I can carry them with me wherever I go. You already carry your purse and school books; will you carry your scriptures? If you will, others will follow your example. You'll discover special friends who will be excited to share with you scriptures that are special to them. I have a friend who often calls me and asks, "Have you got your scriptures there?" With excitement in her voice she'll add, "Let me share with you what I've found." And then she will read a scripture to me. I'll ask, "Where did you find that? What is the reference?" Then I get excited and mark my scriptures. But I had to learn to walk first. As you keep trying, sooner than you realize you'll have a few favorite scriptures marked that you can turn to easily. And you'll love the standard works like special friends. If you do not have your own set of scriptures, will you make a plan to get them?

Let me tell you about an old set of scriptures that my mom and dad gave me when I turned seventeen. I had read the Book of Mormon before, but one day it was different. Perhaps I was more in tune with the Spirit, or maybe I had studied more diligently and prayed more fervently. I was young, but I wanted to know for myself if the Book of Mormon was true. On that particular day I came to the part about faith in the thirty-second chapter of Alma. As I finished that chapter, I experienced a feeling that I recognized as a witness from the Holy Ghost—I knew the Book of Mormon was true. I wanted to stand up and shout. I wanted to tell the whole world what I knew and how I felt, but I was alone. So with tears of joy streaming down my face, I wrote on the margin all the way around the page the feelings in my heart at that moment. I made a big red star in the margin on the top of the page and wrote, "May 31st, 7:30 a.m. This I know, written as if to me." Then I wrote in the margin on one side, "I have received a confirmation. I know the Book of Mormon is true." Across the margin on the other side I wrote, "One month ago I began fasting each Tuesday for a more sure knowledge. This I know."

I am anxious for you too to know and love the scriptures so they can be your comfort when the climb is steep and scary and risky. When you study them diligently, they become *your* scriptures. Like letters from home, they can guide you with feelings of inspiration as you make important choices every day. As you become more and more familiar with the scriptures, they can eventually become your favorite stories, easy to read, and they will help you have determination to stand firm for righteousness even when it's difficult.

Now, will you join me in making a renewed commitment to increase your scripture study? Will you make a plan to have a set of scriptures of your own to keep close and carry with you? Will you accept this invitation, this challenge, to read the scriptures regularly? If you will do this, I promise you that our Father in heaven will draw near to you because you will be drawing near to him. (See D&C 88:63.) You will find peace in your heart with a conviction of his love and nearness that you cannot deny in happy times or troubled times. You live, and one day you will die. And when you do, you will know the Savior, for you will have studied his words, and kept his commandments, prayed fervently and daily, and felt his nearness as he walks with you along the steep and sometimes hard path on our journey home. To this I bear my testimony.

*Faith*

# My Dad Came
# After Me

Every young woman, wherever she is, who is striving for righteousness, can join with a quarter of a million other young women in becoming a mighty force for good. Yes, *you* can bring light where there is darkness, hope where there is despair, and faith where there is doubt. It is not easy, I know. You know it too. I believe it may be as hard as—maybe even harder than—the struggles of our young pioneer sisters who pushed handcarts, suffered extreme fatigue, or were deserted by family or loved ones when they joined the Church.

An account from my great-grandmother's journal gives this example: "Almost a century and a half ago, the Book of Mormon was brought into the home of Susan Kent when she was sixteen years of age. After studying the Book of Mormon, Susan gained a testimony of the truth of the book that was so strong she could not reject it, although to accept it meant a great sacrifice for her. She was at the time engaged to a young man and felt she could not endure being separated from him, but he would have nothing to do with anyone who would join the Mormons. She did not count the cost; she chose the path of peace for her conscience, but her heart was so grieved that she could partake of no nourishment for several days. Then she lapsed into a coma so profound it had the appearance of actual death. Preparations were being made for her funeral until she awoke asking, 'How long have I slept?' With tender care, she slowly regained her health and, with her sister Abigail and their parents, joined the Church." I'll be eternally thankful to my great-

31

grandmother Susan Kent for her testimony of the Book of Mormon and what it meant in her life and now in mine.

In today's world, you will have different kinds of experiences; nevertheless, they will require personal sacrifice. Your challenges will require moral courage to mark a straight and narrow path for others to follow. Your challenges may be similar to Susan's. Perhaps you will have to break an engagement or decline an invitation to a dance or a party because you have chosen to follow the teachings of the Book of Mormon and our modern-day prophet. This is a time when the influence of many movies, fashions, music, and fads would try to desensitize us so that the greatest and most dangerous hazards appear not so bad, and the loud voices of the world would be allowed to interfere with the whisperings of the Spirit within us and thus threaten our eternal life.

Recently a young woman from Texas told about her struggle to be good. She spoke of the constant bombardment of evils made to appear appealing at school, on the TV, and in advertisements. There is hardly an area of life that is protected from messages of immorality. "We simply can't make it alone," she said.

Because of these enticements in the world, we all need to strive together. None of us need travel alone; in fact, we must not if we are to avoid the dangerous hazards along the way. When we strive together in righteousness with our families and friends, there is increased safety. Now some families are more complete than others, but every family is precious. There are times when we need help from our families and don't even know it, and may not even want it, and it doesn't make sense until later. Let me explain what I mean.

One evening years ago, while attending a Sunday School party, I looked at the clock and saw that it was past the time I had been told to be home. Just then a knock came on the door. I was horrified—my father had come after me. I felt humiliated in front of my friends. I thought I wanted to die. I was not pleasant with my father; disobedience never makes one pleasant.

A few years later, some friends and I were driving home from a dance across an Indian reservation ten miles from any shelter. It was forty degrees below zero, and the windchill continued to lower the temperature. A few miles farther into the blizzard we discovered the heater was no longer working; it was frozen up. The car would no longer run, and we came to a slow stop. We watched the snow swirling in front of us only until the windows quickly froze over. Then we were quiet and sober as we contemplated our fate. Our very lives were in danger. The silence was broken as a friend in the back seat asked, "How long do you think it will be before your dad will get here?" Why do you think they thought my father would come? One time I had thought I wanted to die because he came after me; this time we lived because he came through the blizzard to save my life and the lives of my friends. This time I was pleasant with Dad—pleasant and very grateful.

This life provides many causes for disunity and strife. Evil forces are working relentlessly to have us bring contention into our homes over any issue and threaten our happiness, our peace, and our love for each other.

Some time ago a young girl came to my office with anger in her voice and hurt in her eyes. She wanted to tell me all the things she didn't like about her mother. I listened and listened until she got it all out. It was a long list. There was silence; then I asked, "Is there anything good about your mom?" I waited. I think she had refused to let her mind think in that direction until that moment. I asked, "Amy, how do you feel about your mom?" She raised her head, tears streaming down her cheeks, and said, "She is my mom, and I love her." She had discovered love. Now there is no magic formula. She still had to go home and work her problems out day by day, but she let go of the strife in her heart, and now she wanted to strive together with her mother. And that's exactly what her mother had been praying for.

Miracles can happen when we decide to work together. In Amy's case something of a miracle did happen. It's okay that your parents aren't perfect; no parents are. And it's okay that they didn't have perfect children either; no children are. You see, our whole purpose is to strive together in righteousness, overcoming our weaknesses day by day. We must never give up on one another.

Sometimes a daughter can rescue a parent in times of storm when she cares enough to help. I know of a family where the father has had to move from job to job. In his kind of work, many people are getting laid off. He might have come home and called his wife into the other room and said, "My dear, we don't have enough money to pay the bills, but I know how much Julie wants that expensive sweater. I told her we would try to get it for her. I don't

want to disappoint her. What am I going to do?" There might have
been some teenage daughters saying, "But all of the other kids get
new things. We deserve them too. Besides, Dad promised." But that
wasn't the way it happened. The father came home, but he didn't
have to say anything. Julie and her sister knew. Julie didn't say, "Dad,
what are you going to do?" She put her arm around his shoulder and
said, "Oh Dad, we can help." How do you think her father felt? Do
you have any idea how her mother must have felt?

Since that time Julie has been working two jobs, twelve hours a
day, to pay for her college tuition in the fall. On the day her
twelve-year-old brother wanted to go to camp but couldn't because
he had no suitable pants to wear, Julie received her pay from both
jobs. Her mother told me that she held out the money for her tithing,
held back the portion she must save each week for her college
tuition, and had enough left to take her brother shopping for the
much-needed pants. How do you think her brother felt? How do you
think Julie felt?

Disappointment and sacrifice can provide the struggles that
make us pull together or it can become the enemy that will divide
and destroy families. Each of us will decide which it will be.

I am convinced that if each of us will stop, like Amy, and think of
the good things instead of the bad, we will discover that love which
will bind us safely together with our families through all of the
skirmishes that occur with loved ones (like having to share the
bathroom, the car, the one nice dress, or whatever with loved ones
who are not yet perfect—striving together through thick or thin).
And, lest we become anxious, let us remember that perfection is
hard work and comes only a step at a time.

Every Sunday as we partake of the sacrament we promise again
to strive to keep the commandments so the Spirit of the Lord will be
with us always. When we learn to listen to the whisperings of that
Spirit within us and have the courage to follow its promptings, we
will become noticeably different because we won't be doing many
of the things that are popular with the world. It won't be easy, but we
can handle that.

Let me share with you the last lines of a poem written by my
sister Shirley for her children:

*Listen to your inner drummer,*
*Step to its quiet beat;*
*The world beats another rhythm,*
*A rhythm of defeat.*

*We'll become a holy people,*
*Peculiar and divine,*
*Living in the world*
*But walking out of time.*

There will continue to be strife in the world, but because of the covenants or promises we have made to care about one another and the promises our Father in heaven has made never to leave us or desert us, we will come through the storm together to rescue each other in times of danger, even as my father came after me. We will look forward with faith in God, having our hearts knit together in unity and in love one toward another.

We can do this; I know we can.

The evils of our day will increase, even as the wicked armies of Pharaoh threatened the children of Israel in the time of Moses, but with faith in God, striving together in righteousness, we of all people have reason to rejoice and take heart. With our eyes fixed on heaven, we'll watch the Red Sea part.

*Divine Nature*

# Influence, Not Power

In order to realize the full blessings of our Father's plan involving the power and authority of the priesthood, each young man and each young woman must prepare to do their part. While the duties and responsibilities, the influence, and the native endowments of young men and young women are different, I believe their preparation to receive the full blessings of the priesthood is more alike than different.

Let's start at the beginning, at least at the beginning of our earth life, and consider those times when the power and the authority of the priesthood become very important to us personally.

When we entered earth life as tiny infants, we were each blessed and given a name by one holding the authority to act in God's name. We began our earthly mission and our names were recorded on the records of the Church.

This pattern was observed even before the birth of our Savior, when Zacharias and Elisabeth presented their son to receive his earthly name and blessing. The child's name had been revealed to Zacharias by an angel. He was to be known as John, the forerunner of Jesus Christ. By the power of the priesthood, this blessing was given.

When we were baptized and became members of the Church of Jesus Christ, we participated in the first priesthood ordinance in which we made covenants. It opened the way for us to start on the path to our Father in heaven. We were baptized by the same power and authority as John the Baptist exercised when he baptized Jesus Christ, our Savior, in the river Jordan.

The gift of the Holy Ghost follows baptism and constitutes the next essential ordinance of the gospel. We each had hands laid upon our head by one having the authority of the Melchizedek Priesthood, and by that power we were blessed to receive the Holy Ghost. The Holy Ghost can be a companion to us throughout life. The Holy Ghost is given to guide us, teach us, comfort us, inspire us, and bear witness to us of the reality of the Savior and the truths of the restored gospel.

Many of us have had or will have other experiences with the blessings and power of the priesthood and with the gift of the Holy Ghost. Some young people are called and set apart, by one having authority of the Holy Priesthood, to serve as quorum or class officers. When we are set apart, hands are laid on our heads and we receive the power and authority to act in the office to which we are called.

One Laurel president explained it this way: "I was called to be a class president of seventeen girls, and the bishop said I was responsible to help them. I was scared to death. I didn't even know for sure where they were. Then he told me to decide on my counselors and reminded me of the need to pray and ask the Lord. I wondered how it worked—how would I know who the Lord wanted? I wrote seventeen names on a piece of paper," she continued. "Then I prayed about those names. I kept thinking and praying and crossing off names until the third day. With only two names remaining, I had a strong feeling that I knew who Heavenly Father wanted. That's how it works!" (*New Era,* May 1974, p. 14.)

It is appropriate for her and for each of us to recognize and witness the power of the Holy Ghost as we seek inspiration concerning the calls we receive from our Heavenly Father through our bishop.

The power of the priesthood and the importance of its restoration and blessings came to have special meaning in my life when I was just fifteen. My mother and father were miles away from our home, and my grandmother was staying with me. While they were away, a serious ear infection developed, and I was rushed to the hospital. The infection required major surgery, which was carried out immediately. Following the operation, I overheard one of the doctors tell a nurse that the damage to my ear had been so severe that I would permanently lose my hearing and my equilibrium.

When my parents arrived at the hospital and realized the seriousness of my situation, they knew what to do. My father and another Melchizedek Priesthood holder, having the power and authority to act in the name of God, administered to me, using oil that had been consecrated by the priesthood for the healing of the sick. My father placed his hands upon my shaven head, which was mostly wrapped in bandages, and gave me a blessing. My mother was also impressed that she should place my name on the prayer roll of the Alberta Temple, where those in attendance would join their faith in prayer for me. It was the first time I knew that people could have their name placed on the prayer roll in the temple. In time, through faith and the power of the priesthood, my healing was complete.

As a member of the Church, have you felt the power of the priesthood in the administrations and blessings you may have received? Have you received a father's blessing? Have you asked your father to give you a blessing at special times of need—like the beginning of a new school year, or during times of discouragement, or when you are carrying a heavy responsibility, or when you are struggling for understanding? These are times when you can receive that strength which you need. And in the absence of your father, you can ask your home teachers, your bishop, or a special friend who has been ordained to act in God's name. I know that such blessings can be a great comfort to you. They have for me and they can for you.

You are at an age when you are thinking about and making important decisions, sometimes difficult decisions, that will affect the rest of your life. As a member of the Church, you have the privilege to receive another unique priesthood blessing, a patriarchal blessing. This blessing can be given to you, upon your request and worthiness, by a patriarch ordained of God to this special calling. A patriarchal blessing can serve as a guide to you with promises that are predicated upon your faithfulness in keeping the commandments. When I was sixteen, Brother Anderson, our stake patriarch, placed his hands on my head and declared my lineage and gave me a patriarchal blessing. This blessing has been a tremendous strength to me throughout my life. Through the years, when unanswered questions have weighed heavily on my mind, I have read and reread my blessing hundreds of times. It has been an anchor, a comfort, and a guide to me. Through the authority of the priesthood, a patriarchal blessing can be yours also to guide you and help you throughout your life.

Another of the great priesthood ordinances designed to bless us was instituted by the Savior when the final hours of his earthly ministry were approaching. During his last supper with his apostles, he blessed some bread, broke it in pieces, and passed it on to them, saying, "Take, eat; this is in remembrance of my body which I give as ransom for you." He then took a cup and gave thanks and passed it to them, saying, "Drink ye all of it. For this is in remembrance of my blood of the new testament, which is shed for as many as shall believe on my name, for the remission of their sins." (JST Matthew 26:22–24.)

Each Sunday young men who hold the Aaronic Priesthood prepare and administer the sacred ordinance of the sacrament. For the sake of order and wise government, our Heavenly Father has bestowed the priesthood and accompanying administrative responsibilities upon his sons. While it is the duty of the Aaronic Priesthood holders to prepare and pass these sacred emblems, every worthy member is privileged to partake and to receive the blessings promised in this priesthood ordinance.

It is also by the authority of the priesthood that both young men and young women are set apart to be messengers of truth and teach the gospel when they receive calls from a prophet of the Lord to serve as missionaries for The Church of Jesus Christ of Latter-day Saints.

Likewise, in the House of the Lord, the temple, all things are done by the power and authority of the priesthood. In the temple, men and women are endowed and make sacred priesthood covenants that are accompanied by promises and blessings. One day every righteous young man and woman will have the privilege and opportunity—if not in this life, in the eternities—for a celestial marriage and an eternal family. The highest blessings of the priesthood are conferred only upon a man and a woman together in the temple. This priesthood ordinance is necessary for exaltation in the highest degree of the celestial kingdom. As the Apostle Paul said, "Neither is the man without the woman, neither the woman without the man, in the Lord." (1 Corinthians 11:11.) They are truly partners in priesthood blessings.

And so we come together and rejoice together as we recount the blessings we each receive as a result of the priesthood. It is a power that blesses us daily and prepares us for eternity.

Through the restoration of the Church in this dispensation, priesthood ordinances and covenants that set young men and young women apart from the world are available to each person. This is according to our Heavenly Father's plan. The preamble to the Young Women Values states that young women are to prepare to make and keep sacred covenants, receive the ordinances of the temple, and enjoy the blessings of exaltation.

We are well acquainted with the duties and responsibilities of young men who hold the Aaronic Priesthood. But what of our young women? What is their calling? President Spencer W. Kimball said, "To be a righteous woman is a glorious thing in any age. To be a righteous woman during the winding-up scenes on this earth before the Second Coming of our Savior is an especially noble calling. A righteous woman's influence can be tenfold what it might be in more tranquil times." (*Ensign*, November 1978, p. 103.)

How can a woman use her influence in this calling? How can she use it in righteousness? Let me tell you what one young woman did. Following her decision to take a stand for truth and righteousness in a very difficult situation, she received a letter from an older friend, which read: "I just wanted to apologize for last night. I was proud to see you holding your standards and not just going along with the crowd which is so easy to do. I want you to know that you made me think twice and reevaluate my own standards on immoral, R-rated movies. Your example has made me want to try harder in listening to the Church's counsel on this matter. I'm sure the Lord is proud of you. Thank you for your friendship."

Age is not a limitation. Each of us has a significant calling. Each young woman, magnifying her calling to become a righteous woman, as this one did, can help thwart the powers of the adversary, deter the proliferation of pornography, and guard against immorality. Our righteous influence can affect many things—the degree of love and harmony in our homes, the number of young people proclaiming the gospel, the behavior of a friend, the atmosphere in our classrooms and workplaces. Elder Russell M. Nelson has said to young women of every age, "Your powerful influence for good is needed today as never before. A righteous young woman's influence is great."

How do we prepare, as a prophet has said, to be ten times more influential than we might be in more peaceful times? (See Spencer W. Kimball, *Ensign,* November 1978, p. 103.) Our preparation comes as we learn who we are and what we are to do. The Young Women Values can guide us in this preparation. To the question "Who am I?," the values of Faith, Divine Nature, and Individual Worth teach us that we are all daughters of a Heavenly Father who loves us. We have inherited divine qualities. We are each of infinite worth with our own divine mission.

To the question, "What am I to do?," the values of Knowledge, Choice and Accountability, Good Works, and Integrity will help guide us. As we "continually seek opportunities for learning and growth," we will increase our knowledge and testimony of the gospel. We will be strengthened in our desire always to choose good over evil and to accept responsibility for our choices. We will learn to nurture others and play a major part in building the kingdom of God through righteous service, beginning within our own families. And finally, we will develop the moral courage to make our actions always consistent with our knowledge of right and wrong, allowing us to stand as witnesses for Christ "at all times and in all things and in all places." (Mosiah 18:9.)

As we study the Young Women Values with their scriptural references, they will help prepare us to exert a righteous influence. And as we use the values as guides to live by each day, the Lord will strengthen us and his Spirit will bring a marvelous awakening within us. We will begin to understand what it means to become a "light in the Lord" and to "walk as children of light." (Ephesians 5:8–9.)

Sometimes I have walked at dusk in the hills near my home. I watch the sun setting in the west over the lake and the shadows lengthening until the most familiar landmarks around me are gradually obscured in the darkness. I suddenly feel alone and a little unsure. But then a little miracle occurs. One by one the lights begin appearing—in the houses, along the streets, and even in the surrounding darkness—and I regain my sense of direction. Reassured and cheered by their brightness, I make my way safely home.

Each of us is like those lights. In a world of increasing darkness, when the adversary is doing all in his power to eliminate light and obscure every familiar landmark, the Savior's words lovingly implore, "Hold up your light." (3 Nephi 18:24.)

It is not power and authority but rather the strength of our light, our great example, and our influence that will significantly affect the spiritual growth of the Church in the last days.

"Women are appointed . . . to be guides and lights in righteousness," said Elder Bruce R. McConkie. (*Ensign*, January 1979, p. 63.) I promise you that as you follow the Savior's example, live the principles of the gospel, and stand for truth and righteousness, you will become light- and life-giving. This is the glorious mission of young women.

# Who Are You
# Anyway?

Late one afternoon in the San Jose, California, airport, people were milling around, waiting for the luggage to appear on the carousel, with few seats available for waiting. The usual airport noises added to the restlessness of the impatient travelers. A group of strangers, we were each interested in our own destinations.

Against the wall near the outside door, an elderly woman sat hunched over on one of the few benches in the waiting room, a couple of boxes tied with string tucked next to her feet. I moved over near her and watched. She seemed not to notice me. She wrung her frail hands, spotted with age, over and over again, while deep lines furrowed her face. Many people walked by with little notice as she kept a steady watch on the outside door.

Taking a few steps closer, I asked, "Could I be of any help to you?" She looked up, startled, then said, "I'm supposed to meet my daughter out in front. She said she would come and pick me up, but I don't know where to go, and I can't carry my things."

Together we got through the big door with her packages and found a bench near the area where people were being picked up. I wondered how long she had been waiting, and if her daughter knew how frightened and unsure her mother was in this unfamiliar place. Might better arrangements have been made for this elderly woman who seemed so alone, frightened, and unsure? The anxious traveler slowly sat down once again and pulled her packages close to her.

Looking up through her wire-rimmed glasses, she asked, "Who are you anyway? You must be somebody."

I told her my name and then asked this stranger bent with age and the care of years, "Who are you?" "Oh, I'm nobody," she said. *Nobody?* I thought. *You're somebody's mother and you're . . .* At that moment a car pulled up, and a middle-aged woman in fine clothes got out of the driver's seat and hurried toward the elderly woman. "That's her. That's my daughter," the mother told me.

The daughter, without taking time for a greeting or welcome, grabbed her mother's arm and hurried her toward the car, too fast for the comfort of tired and worn-out legs. Maybe her impatience had something to do with her concern for being double-parked. I hoped that was the explanation for her impatience. When the mother was seated in the car, the daughter returned to the bench and picked up the two boxes, which looked quite out of place with her appearance and her fine car. Then she got in the driver's seat, her mother in the seat beside her with her head barely peeking above the window, and together they drove away.

Since that day in San Jose, I hear ringing in my ears a tired voice, saying, "Oh, I'm nobody." Just how many nobodies are there in this world? And how many somebodies? And how do you tell the difference?

In London, England, on a beautiful day in April, that question popped into my mind again. We arrived at Heathrow Airport and took a taxi to our hotel by way of Buckingham Palace. It was three o'clock in the afternoon, and large numbers of people were moving toward the palace. As we rode down the street opposite the palace entrance, we saw uniformed policemen mounted on beautiful black horses. Lines of school children in navy uniforms with brass buttons, looking as official in their uniforms as the officers of the law, were carrying beautiful bouquets of bright yellow daffodils. "Surely this is not a regular occurrence," I said, and the taxi driver informed me that it was a celebration for Queen Elizabeth's birthday. The celebration was to begin at four o'clock, when the children would gather in front of the great palace and begin singing. Fifteen minutes later the Queen of England, Queen Elizabeth II, would appear on the balcony and everyone could participate in this historic event by singing happy birthday to her.

In my mind, I remembered my childhood and how my grandmother who came from England would recite a nursery rhyme to
me: "Pussy cat, pussy cat, where have you been? I've been to London
to visit the queen. Pussy cat, pussy cat, what did you there? I
frightened a little mouse under a chair." I remembered the many
times my mother told me about the queen and that I could be like a
princess if I did all the things a princess should do—"like using
good table manners even when you're eating all by yourself," she
would say. She read to me about how the queen's dresses have little
weights in the hemline so that if she is in public and the wind blows,
she will never be seen in an unqueenly situation. My sisters and I
collected pictures of the queen and made scrapbooks. And in my
hometown in Canada, almost every public gathering was closed by
the congregation singing "God Save the Queen."

You can be sure that at four o'clock, I was at Buckingham Palace,
the very palace we had gathered pictures of years before. I looked
around at the people—young and old, poor and well-to-do. I
watched as they stood with eyes riveted on the balcony, which was
decorated with red, white, and blue bunting. At four o'clock the
children began to sing. Fifteen minutes later a hush fell over the
crowd. The balcony doors opened, and out stepped six uniformed
buglers in fancy attire. They raised their instruments, with long
banners hanging from each horn, and played a stirring fanfare. Then
the people in the courtyard cheered as the queen came into view.
She was dressed in a bright yellow suit, and as if by signal, the
children waved their bright yellow daffodils and sang the special
birthday song. The queen waved to the people, many of whom had
tears in their eyes. Quite by surprise I wiped tears from my own eyes,
thinking about the history of this royal family—their nobility, their
example, their service to their country, their loyalty, and their royalty.
There stood the Queen of England, a real somebody surrounded by
her subjects, her kingdom, and her empire.

I supposed no one had ever asked Queen Elizabeth, "Who are
you?" If they had done so, everyone could answer, "She is the Queen
of England." No more would need to be said.

Is it power and authority, popularity, prestige, and position that
makes one a somebody? My mind raced by from the Buckingham
Palace in London to the airport in San Jose, from the Queen of
England to the elderly woman who told me, "Oh, I'm nobody."

In the book *Roots,* author Alex Haley says, "In all of us there is a hunger, marrow-deep, to know our heritage, to know who we are and where we have come from. Without this enriching knowledge, there is a hollow yearning. No matter what our attainments in life, there is still a vacuum, an emptiness, and the most disquieting loneliness."

When we know who we are, we have a great sense of well-being, a purpose for being, a reverence for life, and a sense of whom we have the capacity to become. President George Q. Cannon, a counselor in the First Presidency nearly a century ago, taught, "We are the children of God, and as His children there is no attribute we ascribe to Him that we do not possess, though they may be dormant or in embryo." (*Gospel Truth,* Deseret Book, 1974, 1:1.)

Elder Bruce R. McConkie has told us something about becoming queens: "If righteous men have power through the gospel and its crowning ordinance of celestial marriage to become kings and priests to rule in exaltation forever, it follows that the women by their side (without whom they cannot obtain exaltation) will be *queens* and priestesses. Exaltation grows out of the eternal union of a man and his wife." (*Mormon Doctrine,* Bookcraft, 1966, p. 613.)

I wanted to tell the old woman in San Jose that she could become a queen. I wanted to tell her about the gospel of Jesus Christ. I wanted to tell the Queen of England that she too could become a queen—not just the Queen of England, but a queen forever in God's kingdom. I want every woman—young or older—who feels that she is a nobody, and everyone who feels that she is a somebody, to know that in the gospel of Jesus Christ every woman can become a queen through the ordinance of celestial marriage in the holy temples of God.

As I watched the crowds of people at the Queen's birthday, I wished I could stand on the balcony of Buckingham Palace and shout to every young woman within the sound of my voice, "You are a somebody!" Then I would tell them about the Young Women Values. If it were possible, I wish that I could talk to every young woman personally. I would say, "You are a daughter of a Heavenly Father who loves you and who has an eternal plan for you that is centered in Jesus Christ your Savior." I would tell her that she has a divine nature and has inherited divine qualities. I would tell her of her individual worth, her infinite worth, with her own divine mission and the promise of exaltation through sacred ordinances and covenants in the House of the Lord. I would ask every young woman in The Church of Jesus Christ of Latter-day Saints to ask everyone she meets if they have heard, and, if not, to shout it loud and clear: No one is a nobody! Everyone is a somebody in our Heavenly Father's kingdom! We are all daughters of God.

"And now, because of the covenant which ye have made ye shall be called the children of Christ, his sons, and his daughters; for behold, this day he hath spiritually begotten you; for ye say that your hearts are changed through faith on his name; therefore, ye are born of him and have become his sons and his daughters." (Mosiah 5:7.)

# You Are One
# Terrific Person

It was our last day in Hawaii, and I had carefully selected several gifts to take to my family at home. I already had several small gifts for five-year-old Kent, but I could not resist buying a T-shirt that caught my eye as we were waiting in the airport. When we arrived home and opened our luggage to hand out the various souvenirs to the children in our family, the gift that received the greatest response was the T-shirt presented to Kent.

At first it appeared to be just another T-shirt, of which he had plenty, but when his sister read the message printed on the front, it became much more. Kent immediately pulled and pulled to get his shirt over his head, ready to replace it with this gift with big letters in bright colors that read "Inside this Hawaiian shirt is one terrific kid." He smoothed the shirt over his chest and stomach and walked around proudly for everyone to see. It was obvious that this statement worn so boldly made him feel he was one terrific kid, and with the T-shirt on, he had the evidence to prove it. He ran out to the neighbors' homes to show his friends. That night he slept in his new T-shirt.

The next afternoon, after he had played outside all morning, Kent's mom suggested that he change his shirt. He agreed only after she gave in to his request that she wash it immediately and then put it in the dryer so he could wear it again as soon as possible.

One evening a couple of weeks later, when I agreed to take care of Kent while his parents were away for a few hours, I was surprised to see him wearing his special T-shirt. By now it was showing signs of considerable wear. He didn't need anyone to read the message on the front. He knew what it said and was anxious to remind me. Pointing to his chest, he announced with confidence, "Inside this Hawaiian shirt is one terrific kid," and I agreed.

When I got him ready for bed, together we pulled the shirt over his head. Then he folded it carefully ready for another day. I thought to myself, what if that message, which seems to increase his confidence, could be written on his skin so he could wear it always, so he would never take it off and would always be reminded that he is a terrific boy.

I rubbed his bare back. "Kent," I said, "this shirt of skin is made of fine material." He laughed and said, "Rub it some more." I continued to rub his back and to explain. "This shirt of skin is washable and it grows with you. You will never outgrow it. If you fall down and get a hole in it, such as when you skin your knee, it will even mend itself without a needle or thread. It is really very fine. It's like a coat of skin, and you look wonderful in it."

Often since that evening together, Kent has asked me to tell him about his coat of skin and how inside that coat of skin is one terrific kid. I want him to know that when his T-shirt wears out or when he grows out of it, he is still the same wonderful little boy inside.

Sometimes, even when we get older, some people feel they need to wear certain clothes that they believe will tell their friends that they really are special. Many years ago, when I was in high school, it seemed to me that all of the girls who were popular wore certain brands of clothes. I thought that if I could just own a sweater and a pair of shoes with the right brand names, I would never ever lack confidence or feel unsure again.

Today, just as when I was young, many young women want to wear the "right" labels. In fact, manufacturers are so aware of how important labels are that they even sew them on the outside of clothing, so everyone can see what brand you are wearing. Of course, stores can charge very high prices for popular brands. Sometimes the quality of brand-label clothing is really worth the extra money, but often it is just the label that costs so much, a label gives a person the message: "If I wear this brand, I'm special."

One young woman actually saved her meager lunch money for weeks and went hungry each day because she was starving for the confidence she thought she could buy with a certain brand of T-shirt with a little brand symbol on the front. Another young woman was reported to have sold the label from her old shirt to a friend who couldn't afford to buy that brand but who thought she would feel better if she could sew even an old label in the neck of her sweater.

Oh, what a plight the merchants and fashion designers would be in if the truth were ever known and everyone understood about their own coat of skin, that marvelous covering that is always with us and can never be taken off. When we understand its divine nature, we can be reminded that inside the coat of skin of each individual is one wonderful human soul. While we may decide by choice or circumstance to wear clothes without popular labels, we can radiate a confidence that may even cause people to ask, "What brand is your outfit?" And we might answer with a smile, "You mean my coat of skin? I call it Divinity." If there is further question, we might refer them to Webster's dictionary: "Divinity: The quality or state of being divine; goddess."

When we each discover who we really are and the reality of our divine nature, we will always be anxious to look our very best and act our very best. Our confidence will come not from the labels we are wearing but rather from what is inside. Our knowledge of our divine nature and our individual worth helps us understand what the Psalmist meant when he said, "What is man, that thou are mindful of him? and the son of man, that thou visitest him? For thou hast made him a little lower than the angels, and hast crowned him with glory and honour." (Psalm 8:4–5.)

To every young woman I would say, on days when your confidence is low and your dress is not the very latest fashion, just close your door, talk to your Heavenly Father, and tell him you need extra courage and confidence this day. Before leaving the privacy and security of your own room, stop long enough to repeat the first three Young Women Values:

"*Faith:* I am a daughter of a Heavenly Father who loves me, and I will have faith in his eternal plan, which centers in Jesus Christ, my Savior.

"*Divine Nature:* I have inherited divine qualities which I will strive to develop.

"*Individual Worth:* I am of infinite worth with my own divine mission which I will strive to fulfill."

Now you are ready for the day, and whatever label you are wearing or not wearing will make little difference if you remember who you really are inside your wonderful coat of skin.

Live for the day when you will be privileged to go to the temple, the House of the Lord, and from that day forward you will have a special garment to wear. When you fully understand, you will draw strength from that blessing and, like Kent, will want to wear that garment night and day.

*Divine Nature*

# The Gift

Late in the evening, the Christmas lights sparkled like jewels in the night as we left the city and drove through the snow-packed streets to the outskirts of town. The lights were not as plentiful here, but each colorful bulb added beauty to the more humble homes nestled together in the gently falling snow. Driving down one street and then another, we tried, with difficulty, to read the snow-covered street signs. Finally we found the address we were looking for, with the house numbers above the front door protected by an overhanging roof. Filling the front window was a huge Christmas tree, which gave privacy to the living room with the curtains drawn wide.

Making our way through the deep snow of the unshoveled walk, we rang the doorbell and were immediately greeted by Brent, an eight-year-old boy. He invited us in. The living room was small but warm and cozy, with a fire burning in the fireplace. The boy's eighty-six-year-old grandfather rested on the couch near the tree with his leg in a cast. He had slipped off the roof while attempting to shovel the heavy snow that had fallen the night before. We had heard of the accident and were anxious to see him at this Christmastime.

While we exchanged greetings and hugs, Brent stood anxiously waiting for the first opportunity to ask a question. In a most forthright and direct way he simply asked, "Have you ever shaken hands with the prophet?" The eagerness with which he asked gave me reason to believe that he may have rehearsed that question in his mind several times in anticipation of my visit.

"Yes, Brent," I said. "I have shaken the hand of the prophet."

"Oh," he said. His eyes were wide, and his voice reminded me of what a great privilege that is. "If I could just shake the hand of the prophet," he went on. His tone suggested that should that be a possibility, it would surely be the greatest Christmas gift he could have; and if not the greatest, at least it would be among the very top.

Sensing the love and respect Brent obviously felt for our prophet, and wanting to somehow provide a tie between the prophet and the young boy, I reached out my hand. "Brent," I said, "this hand has shaken the hand of the prophet."

He grabbed my hand and shook it vigorously. Then, letting go, he turned his hand over from front to back to examine it thoroughly. "I'll never wash my hand," he said. Considering the problems this decision might cause, I suggested that he probably should wash his hand and just keep the memory in his mind. This suggestion was not acceptable. He had a better idea. "Okay," he said, "I'll wash my hand, but I'll save the water." That seemed like a good suggestion, although I supposed he was only joking. Shortly Brent left the room. The warmth from the fire and the lights from the tree created a wonderful setting to visit. Together with Brent's adopted grand-father and his grandmother, we shared memories of Christmases past.

A few minutes later Brent returned, this time carrying a plastic bag dripping with water. Before anyone could question him, he proudly announced, "I washed my hand," holding up the bagful of water for all to see. We talked about the water in the bag and how that was a distant connection to the prophet; then our visit about Christmases past continued. Brent sat on the floor facing the Christ-mas tree, his knees peeking through his faded bluejeans, and from the corner of my eye I watched him examine the bag of water as if he were expecting to see some evidence that this was holy water. The fire burned low and the lights on the tree seemed to brighten.

After a few minutes Brent got up and, taking his treasure with him, left the room. While I wondered if we would see him again before we left, he returned—this time without the plastic bag full of water. He had determined a better solution for his desire to be in touch with the prophet. Standing in the doorway with his T-shirt wet all the way down the front, he explained what he had done. "I drank the water," he said.

This creative solution was not to be viewed as a joke or some-

thing to be made fun of. Brent was serious. He was carrying something important not on the outside, where he could lay it down, but
on the inside. The water from the hand that he had washed that had
shaken the hand of someone who had shaken the hand of the
prophet was now part of him on the inside, and he would keep it. He
seemed very pleased with his solution.

Would it really make any difference? I wondered. What did it
really mean to Brent? It was much more than water, I was sure, but in
the rush of the Christmas season the incident slipped from my mind
until a few days later. Then, at sacrament meeting on the Sunday
before Christmas, I received some understanding of what this young
boy, just recently baptized, was feeling and wanting.

The sacramental prayer had been offered, and the sacred emblems were being passed quietly and reverently. The Sunday before
Christmas brings a sensitivity that makes important things even
more important—a time of recommitment and rededication, of
sorrow for wrong-doings and resolve and hope to do better in the
new year. As the sister on my right passed the sacrament tray and
held it while I raised the small cup of water to my lips, into my mind
came this thought: "I want to get this water on the inside." I thought
of Brent, a newly baptized member. I remembered the baptismal
covenant. I thought of the symbolism of the water, the washing away
of our sins. The cup of water of which I would partake renewed the
promises and blessings of the atonement of Jesus Christ. It was his
birthday we were celebrating. I could hear in my mind again the
sacramental prayer on the water: "that they do always remember
him, that they may have his Spirit to be with them. Amen."

It was Christmas, a holy celebration in memory of the birth of
Jesus Christ, our Lord and Savior. The symbolism of the water was to
represent his blood, which was shed for each of us so that we might
live and have eternal life. The words of a little verse I had heard many
years earlier came to my mind with new meaning: "Though Christ a
thousand times in Bethlehem be born,/If he is not born in thee thy
soul is still forlorn."

"Thank you, Brent," I said to myself, "for this wonderful gift you
have given me, the increased desire to drink the water—the symbolism of his atonement—to get it on the inside so that I might become
more like him."

When we become more like Christ as we renew our covenants

each week and partake of the bread and drink the water, committing ourselves to keep the commandments, we can have his Spirit to be with us; we will become more like him, and it will show.

Alma asked the members of the church in his time, "Have ye spiritually been born of God? Have ye received his image in your countenances? Have ye experienced this mighty change in your hearts?" (Alma 5:14.) The question is paraphrased in the words of a song by Janice Kapp Perry, "His Image in Your Countenance":

> *Have you received his image in your countenance?*
> *Does the Light of Christ shine in your eyes?*
> *Will he know you when he comes again*
> *Because you will be like him?*
> *When he sees you, will the Father know his child*
> *By his everlasting image in your eyes?*

And one day we will answer, Yes, he will know us. He will know us because we will have not only the water inside but the Spirit of God also burning in our hearts. To the question from Brent, "Have you ever shaken hands with the prophet?" my answer is "Yes, but I've also shaken hands with a little eight-year-old boy, and I've learned important and eternal truths from both—a precious gift."

*Divine
Nature*

# Is There
# Any Way Back?

She sat beside me on the ground with her head down, her fingers picking at the last piece of bark on a small branch. The spongy earth along the creek bed was soft with a thick layer of pine needles and dried leaves accumulated over many seasons. We watched the water bubbling over the shiny rocks, illuminated by the sun filtering through the leaves of the big cottonwood trees. The water in the creek was lower now. The spring runoff had receded, and the gushing sounds of a few weeks ago had quieted to a gentle gurgle.

I'd never seen this young girl before today and had spoken to her only briefly over the telephone that very morning. She had sent me a note through the mail asking me to call. She sounded very troubled. At my insistence she had agreed, reluctantly, that maybe her house wasn't too far away, and she would allow me to drive the several miles to pick her up so we could talk together face to face. She said she would be in the street in front of the house. I told her to watch for a red Honda.

As I made my way to her neighborhood, I noticed a young girl in faded blue jeans get up slowly from the curb. She appeared to be nervous, glancing in both directions. I pulled up beside her, leaned over to open the door, and called her name. She quickly got into the car, then slumped down in the bucket seat and slammed the door a little harder than seemed necessary. I let my foot off the brake and we drove down the narrow street. "Would you like to go anywhere special?" She shook her head. "Then would it be okay with you if we drove to a special place of mine by a creek some distance from here?"

"Yes," she said, not looking up.

"I'm glad you wrote to me," I said, hoping to ease her tension, "because I have something I want to tell you." There was no response on her part, except the nervous popping of her gum. She appeared to be about fifteen years old. She was wearing a generous amount of dark blue eye shadow, and her jaw moved back and forth as she ground her teeth nervously. We drove in silence until we reached the creek.

And now, with the final piece of bark removed from the branch she had been fidgeting with, she tossed it into the creek and began talking. Her tone was at first full of resentment, anger, and doubt. Bit by bit she unloaded the burden of her heart. The sound of the flowing water was a soothing accompaniment to the anguish of her story. I listened. Finally, after many pauses during her long account of suffering and heartache, the remaining drops of torment squeezed out a burden too long carried. And yet, the burden still remained. Telling about it was not enough to provide relief.

Her story was one of sorrow, tragedy, and regret for wrong choices, wrong friends, wrong timing, and wrong places. As she glanced up, her eyes revealed the turmoil, the hurt, and the hope-lessness of her soul. In a different tone than before, she asked searchingly, "Is there any way back? I'm only thirteen." She didn't want a quick, easy answer. She was pleading for truth and help. We watched the water together for a moment until the creek itself seemed to provide a visual aid for this very moment. I picked up a clump of loose dirt and tossed it into the stream. It separated, polluting the stream at that spot, but was soon carried out of sight and then the water was crystal clear once again.

"Yes," I said softly, "there is a way back. There is, there is."

"What do I have to do?" she asked, a small note of hope in her anxious voice.

"Before I tell you what you have to do," I said, "I would like you to understand how and why it works. May I tell you that part first?" She nodded in agreement.

"Will you come with me where I was at this time last year and let us walk together where Jesus walked?" I could feel her spirit, which told me she was ready. "I'll be your guide along the way, and together we'll imagine we're singing the songs, walking the paths, and reading the scriptures as we go, just as I did a year ago." I glanced at her to catch the response to this imaginary journey. She was willing.

"There is Bethlehem," I said as we both fixed our eyes on the water in the stream. "It is the birthplace of our Savior, just five miles from Jerusalem. Can you hear our group singing the last line of that sweet song, 'O Little Town of Bethlehem'? Listen carefully." The creek bubbled in accompaniment: "The hopes and fears of all the years / Are met in thee tonight."

I glanced at my young friend. "That means *all* of our fears— yours and mine. See that sunlit meadow just outside of Nazareth where Jesus spent his childhood. There must have been time for him to play and dream there. He became acquainted with the birds and the flowers, the mustard seed, the fig tree, and all of God's creations. Later on he used them to teach the people so they could understand what he wanted them to know." The water washing over the shiny rocks in the creek bed provided the continuity needed for this imaginary pilgrimage.

"Come and stand by me now on the shores of Galilee. It is Sunday evening. This is the sea of miracles. Jesus was here. He crossed this water many times. He walked on its surface. People were hungry, and he fed them near here. Touch the water with me. It's real. It's all here, and it really happened just as the Bible stories said. And now we're standing on the banks of the Jordan River where it is narrow and swift. We'll walk reverently and quietly here. This is holy ground. This is where Jesus was baptized and the voice of God spoke these words: 'This is my beloved Son, in whom I am well pleased.' (Matthew 3:17.) That happened. It really did, in this very river."

Again the little creek somehow added reality to our experience. The young woman, watching the water, appeared to be listening and hoping. I paused a few moments, then went on.

"Now will you climb with me up the rugged Mount of Olives?" I asked. "Jesus must have climbed this mountain to the very top many times. The people crowded around him. They wanted to be near him and with him. The righteous people followed him and became his disciples. Remember the Primary song?"

> *I think when I read that sweet story of old,*
> *When Jesus was here among men,*
> *How he called little children like lambs to his fold,*
> *I should like to have been with him then.*

The memory of my own longing for that experience as a Primary child filled my voice with emotion. "Everyone who knew him wanted to be with him, and they still do. He loved everyone—everyone—and he still does." I tried to tell her in a way that her heart would believe.

"Let us go down now to the foot of the mountain into the Garden of Gethsemane. It's very quiet. People are speaking in hushed tones or not at all. The gnarled old olive trees are still here, just as they were then. It was on this sacred spot that Jesus Christ, our brother, became our Savior. He suffered and died to atone for us—for you and for me. He really did." I glanced at her as she continued to listen.

"It was here," I explained, "that his sufferings were beyond all mortal comprehension, that the weight of our sins caused him to feel such agony, pain, and heartbreak that he bled from every pore as he suffered in body and spirit."

The memory of standing in that garden and trying to comprehend such suffering and such love was so real. There was silence. I wiped the tears from my eyes as my young friend glanced up.

"He voluntarily took upon himself your sins and mine, because that's how much he loves us," I went on. We listened to the creek and pondered. "His part in this great plan of salvation was essential to our getting back to our heavenly home. It is his great love for us that gives us the strength to struggle and suffer to overcome our sins. It was in this very Garden of Gethsemane that Christ atoned for each one of us. It is Christ's atonement that can, if we will just do our part, save us and rid us of our sins and purify us. Our part is to repent and to do what is right."

There was silence now. Even the stream seemed hushed for a moment. "Can you hear voices singing?" I asked.

> *I stand all amazed at the love Jesus offers me,*
> *Confused at the grace that so fully he proffers me;*
> *I tremble to know that for me he was crucified,*
> *That for me, a sinner, he suffered, he bled and died.*

By now her tension had eased; she was relaxed, her spirit anxious. "We know the Son of God knows our struggles and even understands them, all of them. Even though he was perfect, he suffered pains and afflictions of every kind so that he would know exactly how we would feel. In this way he can help us with our most difficult struggles. He didn't have to suffer for us, but he did so because of his great love for us and his obedience to the plan of God, his Father and our Father. And when we make mistakes, even big ones, and feel like pulling away, the great promise of the atonement that took place in the Garden of Gethsemane is offered to us so that we can qualify to return to our heavenly home and have eternal life and live with him some day."

The sound of the water increased, as if in testimony to the great eternal truth. I then repeated these words we know so well:

> *I am a child of God, and he has sent me here,*
> *Has given me an earthly home with parents kind and dear.*
>
> *Lead me, guide me, walk beside me,*
> *Help me find the way.*
> *Teach me all that I must do to live with him someday.*
>
> *I am a child of God, rich blessings are in store;*
> *If I but learn to do his will I'll live with him once more.*

The afternoon breeze began stirring the tiny leaves on the quaking aspen. I turned to my young friend and asked, "Do you remember the third Article of Faith, which says: 'We believe that through the atonement of Christ, all mankind may be saved, by obedience to the laws and ordinances of the Gospel'?" She nodded. "Do you understand better now how it works and why you must go through the steps of repentance, and even suffer in your way?" She nodded again.

We talked about her visit to the bishop, and how anxious he would be to help her unload this heavy burden, and how he would give her direction and counsel and love. "Can you talk to your Heavenly Father about this?" I asked.

"I don't know."

"Then may I talk to him about it for you?"

She nodded. Together we knelt on the banks of the little creek that had served us so well during our journey together. It seemed as though even the light breeze was reverent during our earnest prayer.

As she whispered "Amen," the anguished expression on her face was softened. "I think he cares about me," she said.

"He does care for you, enough to die for you," I testified.

# Individual Worth

*Individual
Worth*

# More than
# Seventeen

When I asked Julie how old she was, she told me she was seventeen. Yes, she was seventeen according to her earth life, but she was thousands of years old, taking into account her pre-earth life. She had forgotten the time before her mortal existence. And so it is with each of us. We remember just the few short years we've been here. One day in the great eternal plan, we will remember everything—who we really are and what we are to become. Julie was more than seventeen, and much more important than she realized.

We sat together on my back porch just as the sun was going down. Her sandy-colored hair was brushed back from her face. Her features were not fine and delicate but distinctive and classic. Her clothes were not fashionable or fancy but youthful and comfortable.

Julie slumped down in the chair and stared out across the backyard, past the fence to the lake and far beyond. Her gaze seemed riveted on the sun as it sank on the horizon, giving a final benediction on another day. It was quiet except for the sound of crickets. I knew Julie had a heavy heart, and sometimes the best way to help is to listen. I waited for her to break the silence. Minutes seem like hours when you're waiting. I wanted to listen to her thoughts, her feelings, and her concerns. I wanted her to share some of the burden she seemed to be carrying. It's hard to help carry another's burden if you don't know what it is.

"Julie," I finally asked, "can I help you?"

She shrugged her shoulders. I tried again. "Do you want to talk?"

Since she didn't say no, I supposed she wanted to say yes but didn't know where to begin. Beginning is always the hardest part. Knowing how important the feeling of individual worth is to one's happiness, I asked, "Julie, how do you feel about yourself?"

Without turning her head or blinking an eye, she continued looking straight ahead while tears formed and began running down her suntanned cheeks. I waited. Finally she broke the silence. "If I was just pretty," she said in almost a pleading tone, "then maybe people would like me."

I wanted to start a strong argument defending the reality of her beauty, but I knew that if in her mind she thought she wasn't pretty, it would make little difference that I could see before me the evidence that her opinion of herself was incorrect. This was not a time to disagree.

"What makes you think you're not pretty?" I asked.

She continued staring ahead as the dusk gradually subdued the shapes of the trees and the evening breeze could be felt. "If I was pretty, people would like me," she said.

"Has anyone ever told you that you are not pretty?" I asked.

"No," she said, "but I can see."

"What can you see?" I pressed for an answer.

Now a little impatient, she looked straight at me. "I can see that I'm not pretty. I'm ugly!" Her tears by now were flowing freely, and she made no attempt to hide them. Her secret was out. She was hurting inside because of an idea in her mind that she believed—the idea that she was ugly.

Until Julie could change her thoughts about herself, I knew in her mind she would always be ugly. She had convinced herself of that. I realized that it was not her looks that needed change, but her thoughts, her false opinion of herself. She had been telling herself the wrong things. She had listened to her own messages, and they had gradually undermined her confidence. I continued to listen to her story until finally darkness closed in on another day of earth life with all of its challenges, blessings, and struggles.

"I'm not pretty," she said again. "Why should I try? It's no use."

I resisted the impulse to interrupt and disagree. She continued: "Nothing ever goes right no matter what I do. Nobody likes me, and sometimes I wish I hadn't been born." She buried her face in her hands.

I knew that if I were to help Julie, it would be by helping her change her thoughts about herself. Disagreeing with her was not the answer, and to deny her feelings would only add to the problem by causing her to feel that I didn't care either. I thought and thought. How do you convince a person against her own convictions? I had an idea. It might not help—but maybe it would.

"Julie," I said, "would you let me share an experience with you that I had some time ago, even though at first it may seem that it has no bearing on your problem?"

"Okay," she said in a tone that seemed to say *If you want to.* I began.

A number of years ago I was on a Church assignment in Korea. On Monday no meetings were scheduled, so Sister Till, the mission president's wife, graciously offered to take me to town to the open marketplace to see the stalls and hundreds of people selling and buying. I had been impressed with the Korean people and was anxious to better understand their habits and traditions. We milled around the marketplace, observing the different sights and sounds and smells. Then Sister Till suggested a visit to a factory where we might want to make a few purchases.

We walked some distance to the factory, which was in an old warehouse. Inside, we found row after row of tables piled high with wooden boxes in many shapes and all carved out of wood. The varied designs on top of the boxes appeared, through the dust, to be made of shells. Sister Till asked if I'd be interested in buying one of the boxes. "I don't think so," I said. They didn't appear to be anything I would want, and I wouldn't use one as a gift for anyone. We stopped at one table and brushed off the dust, exposing a lacquered finish that to me appeared cheap. Sister Till gently suggested that I really should buy at least one, and if I had no use for it, I could give it away. Since she had been so kind to take me shopping, I felt that for only seventeen dollars I should buy at least one as a courtesy, if nothing else. I randomly picked up a box and paid my money, and we left to continue our walk through the marketplace. Back at the mission home, I tucked the box away in my luggage; and when I returned home, I tucked it away in a closet and forgot about it.

One day months later, I visited a friend who was working at a very elegant gift shop. While I waited for her to finish with a customer, I looked around at the beautiful displays of exquisite gifts from all over the world. Suddenly I saw a box that looked amazingly similar to the box I had bought in Korea. I wondered, Could this possibly be the same as my box? After careful examination, I determined there might be such a possibility. The box was resting on a glass case, with a mirror at the back exposing the piece from all sides. A light above reflected off the pieces of inlay on the top of the hexagon-shaped box. As I carefully studied this item that was displayed so artistically in this elegant store, my friend returned and commented, "It's a beautiful piece, isn't it? We get them from Korea." She picked up the box and said, "Notice the craftsmanship in this piece. It is made of a special kind of wood found only in Korea. Notice the skill with which this exquisite mother-of-pearl has been inlaid, making such an artistic design." Even the design looked somewhat familiar to me, though I had not really paid much attention while shopping in Korea. "Just run your finger across the surface," she continued, demonstrating how smooth it felt to the touch. "It has more than ten coats of lacquer that are carefully applied and hand rubbed between each coat. This piece sells for 150 dollars—really a good buy for such artistry and craftsmanship." I had to agree with my friend. I felt that I would gladly have paid 150 dollars for this piece. It appeared to me to be worth it.

By now Julie must have been wondering what this had to do with our discussion. I invited her to come into the house to the living room and to sit on the couch. There on the table before her was a hexagon-shaped box decorated with inlaid mother-of-pearl. The top had ten coats of lacquer, hand rubbed. I handed the box to Julie, and she ran her fingers across the smooth surface and smiled.

"Do you know why the box isn't in my closet anymore?" I asked. "Because you think it's pretty," she replied. "And what do you think?" I asked. "It *is* pretty," she said, examining it very carefully. It was a duplicate of the very box my friend had taken time to tell me about in the gift shop.

"You see," I said, "I didn't recognize the quality. I didn't understand the care taken in the creation. I had not given attention to the intricacy of the design. Not until I saw it as a single box apart from all the rest, in a store where my friend opened my eyes to its value, did I have any appreciation for this beautiful piece. Julie," I asked, "what do you think changed its worth?"

She responded, "The box didn't change. It just looked different to you."

"But how could that be?" I asked. "How did my opinion change?"

She looked thoughtful, so I tried to explain.

"You see," I said, "I had looked at the box in Korea, but I didn't really see it. It wasn't until my friend opened my eyes to its real beauty that it had real value for me. When I understood how it was created, and I saw the price it brought in her shop, my appreciation for the value of my piece changed. I went home and retrieved it from the closet and really saw it for the first time. Now it has this special spot in my home."

I paused a moment, then went on. "When we learn about the worth of something and the price paid for it, we begin to better understand its real value. You see, Julie, you really are very beautiful, and someday when you learn more about your divine nature, you will begin to understand the depth of your own worth. Peter taught us, 'Be partakers of the divine nature, . . . giving all diligence, [and] add to your faith virtue; and to virtue knowledge; and to knowledge temperance; and to temperance patience; and to patience godliness; and to godliness brotherly kindness; and to brotherly kindness charity.' [2 Peter 1:4–7.] Just as my friend opened my eyes to discover the value of the little box from Korea, I would like to be your friend who will help you to see the reality of your own value. Until you learn to feel good about yourself, you'll never be able to believe that people like you, and you'll never believe that you are pretty even if you are."

It was late now, and Julie knew her mother would be concerned about her. She always was. There hadn't been much communication between them, and when Julie had left home, she hadn't told her mother where she was going. She didn't really feel that anyone cared.

"Before you go, Julie," I asked, "will you try a little experiment for just three weeks and then come back and we'll talk again?"

She smiled and said, "What is it?"

"I want you to try very hard to never say discouraging things to yourself," I explained. "That is called 'self talk,' and your mind believes what you tell it. When you say things like 'I'm not pretty, so why try,' you contribute to feelings of self-doubt and self-depreciation. I remember reading once that self-depreciation is a sin." I picked up some sheet music. "Every time negative thoughts about yourself come into your mind, stop and think of the words to this song. I wish I could sing well, and I'd sing for you; but since I can't, I'd like to just repeat the words. Listen carefully and then tell me how you feel."

I repeated the words to the song "I Am of Infinite Worth," which was written by Joy Sanders Lundberg, with music by Janice Kapp Perry:

> *All I need do is remember*
> *If ever I wonder if I am of worth,*
> *Remember my Savior, what He did for me*
> *When He lived among men on this earth.*
> *Pain and unspeakable sorrow*
> *He bore for my sins in Gethsemane.*
> *Then He gave up His life as He hung on the cross,*
> *And He did it all for me.*
>
> *Lovingly Jesus is watching.*
> *He knows I am worth all He suffered for me.*
> *Now I must fulfill my own mission in life,*
> *Ever following Him faithfully.*
> *Line upon line I am striving,*
> *Not seeking the honor or praise of mankind.*
> *I will reach for the joy of Celestial rewards*
> *'Til all that God offers is mine.*
>
> *For I am of worth, of infinite worth.*
> *My Savior, Redeemer, loves me.*
> *Yes, I am of worth, of infinite worth.*
> *I'll be all He wants me to be.*
> *I will praise Him, I will serve Him,*
> *I will grow in His love and fulfill my divine destiny.*
> *For my Savior, Redeemer, loves me.*

"Julie," I said, giving her a copy of the words to the song, "will you memorize the words to this song, and every night before you say your prayers will you repeat the words, and every morning while you are getting ready for school, will you say them over again?"

"Yes," she said, looking at the words.

"And just one more thing: Will you listen to the messages you are telling yourself, and every time you begin to think something in your mind that would lessen your opinion of yourself, will you stop and repeat the chorus? Will you do that?" I asked.

"Yes, I will," she promised.

As we walked toward the front door, we stopped and stood together in front of a mirror on the wall. The light from a nearby lamp magnified the beauty of her distinctive and classic features. One of a kind. A creation divine in nature. A person of individual worth. I asked, "Are you prettier now than when you came tonight?" Julie smiled at herself in the mirror. Maybe she was, for the first time in months and months.

# I Didn't Make
It—or Did I?

"I had always wanted to be a cheerleader," Kay declared. "Some people like to play the piano and other things, but for me it was cheerleading." Her long, honey-blond hair framed her delicate face as she sat tall in the chair. She crossed one leg over the other and her foot bobbed as she spoke, revealing her excitement.

"People don't realize all the work cheerleaders have to do," she explained. "It's not all fun and games as it may appear." With a smile of confidence she continued, "I was a cheerleader during my junior year, and I found out you have to be very dedicated. You have to really love it and really want to do it, or there is no way you can handle the discipline it requires."

Hardly stopping for a breath, her eyes bright, she went on. "It can't be something you are doing just to be popular. You have to really enjoy it. Being a junior cheerleader is actually a test, because you don't get all the glory and the applause from the audience. That doesn't come until you are a varsity leader." Underlining the depth and intensity of her commitment to her goal to become a varsity cheerleader, she explained, "All my life I've heard that if you really want something and want it badly enough, and if you are willing to work hard enough for it, it will happen." Then, leaning forward with both feet on the floor in front of her, she concluded, "I believe that. I had really worked hard that year, and being a junior cheerleader helped me realize how much I really wanted to be a varsity cheerleader."

The summer months quickly slipped away. Soon the tryouts became a focus of interest for the entire studentbody. Anticipation was high, not only for the participants, but for neighbors, relatives, teachers, and anyone close to a candidate for this coveted honor.

Those who tried out performed first for the official judges appointed by the high school. Candidates successful in obtaining a certain rating from the judges went on to perform before the entire studentbody. Those who failed to achieve a rating high enough were eliminated from the competition, seemingly forgotten. Only in the privacy of the homes where the unsuccessful took refuge was the impact of such results recorded, never to be forgotten. The hurt reached into the hearts of all who cared. No one hurts alone.

Kay leaned back in the chair and reflected for a moment. "I had determined my goal. I had worked hard, and I was prepared." She dropped her head, and her blond hair fell forward, covering her beautifully proportioned profile. Then, as if it was hard to believe, she whispered, "I didn't even make it past the judges."

There was a long pause. "And how did you feel?" I asked quietly.

Kay looked up. She recalled the emotions she had experienced at that never-to-be-forgotten moment. "When you lose after you've worked so hard, you hurt inside really bad. You can't explain it—you just get sick and feel mixed up. I ran out of the school. I just wanted to run and never stop. I felt like dying and thought 'It isn't worth it.' Then I broke down and cried and cried. I couldn't help it."

She paused a moment, then looked up with a faint smile when I asked, "And how did you feel toward the judges?"

"I was unhappy with them, I have to admit. I didn't want to have bad feelings toward anyone, but I was really disappointed. I wanted to be a cheerleader so much. That's what I'd worked for all my life, and I just couldn't understand it. My best friend and I tried out together. She made it past the judges, and when she found out I hadn't made it she said, 'I don't want to be a cheerleader if we can't do it together.' She was willing to give up her place for me. But I didn't want that; I'd never want that. I wouldn't want to take away from her just because I didn't make it."

"How did you feel when you finally returned home, Kay?"

She smiled as she reflected on the support from her family. "They were very disappointed, because they knew how much it meant to me. I know it was really hard for them to see me so disappointed. My mother put her arm around me and hugged me to help me know she really cared. My sisters cried—it was hard for them too. I don't remember exactly what everyone said, but they let me know they knew how important it was to me and that they still loved me whether I was a cheerleader or not.

"I guess the really hard thing was to love myself even if I wasn't a cheerleader," she confessed. "I realized that I had to go back to school the next day, and that my life had to go on." She explained, "When I got to school, all my friends were really supportive. In fact, people I didn't even know came up to me and told me that I should have been chosen. They told me they were circulating a petition to have me try out in front of the entire studentbody and have another chance. I couldn't understand it. I thought, 'Why are they making such a big fuss over this just for me?' Suddenly it really hit me. I stopped hurting and began to think. It's almost worth it to lose, even if it hurts. I found out how many friends I have and how everybody cares." And then she confided, "But I still kept thinking, 'Why did it have to happen to me?' "

"How did the hurt disappear?" I asked.

"Gradually," she said. "Time helps—and prayer. I don't know exactly how, but always when I pray I feel comforted when I get up off my knees. I kept thinking that it must have happened for a reason." She reflected, "My seminary teacher talked to me after tryouts and said, 'Even if there isn't a reason now, maybe someday when you're a mother, your children will be going through the kinds of things you're going through. If you always had things easy, it would be hard for you to understand how they feel and to encourage them. You wouldn't be able to comfort them and help them keep trying.' I think that encouragement helped me the most." She paused as if reviewing again the counsel from her seminary teacher. "Maybe I can help someone else."

Having to face disappointments can sometimes leave lasting scars and kill one's enthusiasm. "Has this experience dampened your spirit?" I asked.

Kay responded, "Oh, no. I'm not like that. No matter how much it hurts, I'll try again and again. I love life. I enjoy being with people. I enjoy being at school. I wouldn't want to change anything I have."

"But what about being a cheerleader?"

"Oh, I still would love to be a cheerleader, because you are in front of everybody and you are able to get everyone involved. But I think a lot of times girls want to be cheerleaders because they think more people will like them. Maybe the best thing for me was finding out how everybody cared—really cared—and liked me even though I wasn't a cheerleader.

"I've learned a lot of other things, too. I've begun to realize that everything doesn't always come the way you want it to, even when you work hard for it. You have to learn to take the bad with the good. These are important lessons, and I'd rather learn them now so I will know how to handle disappointments."

"Kay," I asked, "what would you say to comfort other girls who do not make it past the judges and who suffer similar disappointments?"

"I'd tell them not to give up," she said, sitting tall and confident. "I know how they feel and how they hurt, and I know they think they won't ever try again, but if they do give up and quit trying, they'll never become all that they could become. I don't think I'm any less of a person because I'm not a cheerleader.

"Besides," she added, "who's to say I'd have really enjoyed cheerleading this year? Maybe something would have happened that wouldn't have been good for me. I think my Heavenly Father knows better than I do what's best for me. Sometimes when I think back on that experience, I wonder if maybe I really made it after all."

# Do You Think the Lord Is Proud of Me?

There were many families at Aspen Grove Family Camp that week—grandpas and grandmas, aunts and uncles, cousins, mothers and fathers, brothers and sisters. That first evening, after all the participants had been assigned to small cabins tucked away in the pines and decisions had been made about who should sleep in which bunk, people young and old, in groups of twos and threes, were seen sauntering through the wooded area to explore the sights and sounds and smells in their temporary home in the mountains. As they walked together on the pine-needle carpet, sharing feelings more than thoughts as the shadows crept in on the soft evening breeze, a wonderful bonding began to take place—the kinds of feelings that keep people caring about and loving each other even when they sometimes don't think they like each other.

During the next few days I watched from the little balcony of the Sunrise lodge, where I was staying, all the happenings that occurred near or around the center of camp. From this strategic location I could see the immediate response to the dinner bell that called everyone to the dining room for a family-style meal. It seemed much like at home, I thought: those who were first in line were always first, and those who brought up the rear were the same ones each day. It was almost as though they had been assigned those positions in line, just as they had been assigned specific cabins and beds.

The first evening it was quite apparent that families were grouped together with their own. In fact, several groups had matching T-shirts as if to announce a clear identity either for others to be aware of their shared relationship or maybe to remind the family members of an important membership that bound them together in this summer retreat. By noon of the second day, with activities to interest every age and disposition, the family divisions were less clear. First the younger children, then the teenagers and adults, were stepping over the family circle and eagerly wandering into other groups, enlarging their circle to include new friends.

In the camp was a man named Max. Small of stature, he wore heavy black horn-rimmed glasses held together on one side with a twisted paper clip. They sat at an angle across the bridge of his nose, which may have explained why he tilted his head and walked haltingly. His unshaven face, dark with stubby whiskers, and his unsteady walk set him apart from the others. As I watched him move among the people at the family camp, I wondered about the things that were setting him apart from the group. At first the adults were respectful but distant; it was the children who began to open the circle to let him in. They invited him to play games with them. The fact that he was in his forties made little difference to them. Long after other adults had become weary with the children's games, Max would continue to play with them. His greatest contribution was his constant and enthusiastic encouragement to each child, win or lose. Above the cheers and shouts, you could hear Max calling each person by name, shouting, "You done good!"

In a shaded area next to the main lodge was a Hi-Ball court, which was very popular, particularly in the cool hours of the morning and later afternoon. Hi-Ball is played on a trampoline encased on all sides by a net and divided across the middle, like a tennis court. At each end is an opening, somewhat like a basketball hoop, where competing players try to score baskets with a sponge ball while trying to keep their balance on the trampoline.

The first evening in camp, I had met nine-year-old Sandy, who had volunteered to help me with an assignment in the family-night program. I was impressed with her confidence and willingness to help a stranger, since we didn't know each other at that time. On the third day in camp, when I walked past the Hi-Ball court in the early afternoon, with the sun beating down, I was surprised to see Sandy on one side of the court and Max on the other. Sandy spotted me and cried out, "He has forty-five points and I have nine!" To that enthusiastic announcement, Max stopped jumping long enough to explain, "She's my coach," and then the game continued.

As I continued walking down the tree-lined path, listening to the birds, I pondered the impact of this young coach and the extent of her influence. Then I turned around and returned to the court. I realized that while Sandy was Max's coach, as he had announced, she was also coaching me. I wanted to be closer to her, to learn from her.

She was still cheering Max on, calling out the lopsided score. Then she looked up, saw me, and shouted, "Sister Kapp, will you come and play Hi-Ball with Max?" They continued to play while I considered the invitation. I realized that without the first powerful lesson from this young coach, I might have failed this test by making some excuse about the heat or how tired or busy I was. A question was lying in the balance: Had I learned her great lesson or was I just an observer?

"Will Max play with me?" I asked. His response was immediate. "Sure I will!" he shouted. Without further discussion, I found myself climbing through an opening in the net onto the trampoline.

Sandy instructed me briefly, then climbed out and took a place nearby where she could continue coaching both Max and me. She was now cheering Max every time he made a basket, and cheering me every time I tried. Mastering some skills is harder than might be apparent at first, and while I didn't do very well in making baskets, I was aware that my coach was teaching me to score in ways that are not tallied numerically.

Max continued to make baskets, one after another, and Sandy continued to call out his score encouragingly. It seemed that his successes sustained and even increased his energy level. He jumped higher and higher, his skills increasing each time. "The Lord gave me a talent and I didn't know it!" he called out. Then, proudly pointing to Sandy, he added, "And she is my coach!" Though my own skill level was still low, both Max and Sandy shouted encouragement each time I tried to make a basket. "Good try!" they'd yell.

Having been reminded that we do not all have the same talents and energy, especially if we're out of breath and out of balance, I finally suggested that maybe I had had enough of a lesson for one day. Sandy agreed and came over the court to help me out of the net. Max followed. Summing up his lesson for the day, he repeated enthusiastically, "The Lord gave me a talent and I didn't even know it!" Then, in order to not take undue credit to himself, he pointed at Sandy and said, "And she is my coach!"

Sandy smiled broadly and with great pride as her important role was acknowledged. Little did she know, however, of the impact of her lesson on her other student. As we sat on a bench to put on our shoes, Max turned to me and asked, "Do you think the Lord is proud of me?" My answer came quickly. "Yes," I said, with conviction in my heart; "I'm sure the Lord is proud of you and of Sandy too." I thanked Max and Sandy, then walked alone down the path through the tall pines. Max's words continued to ring in my ears and in my heart: "Do you think the Lord is proud of me?" In a grove of trees alongside a mountain stream, I stopped to replay the game in my mind. Then I asked myself, How well am I playing the real game? Is the Lord proud of me?

I wanted to thank Sandy, my young coach, for teaching me so much. And I wanted to thank Max, the man in camp who was different, for his differences. I vowed in my heart that I would remember their teaching, their example, their coaching, and their cheering me on every time I tried, and next time perhaps I would initiate the invitation to play in the game and use better the talents the Lord has given me.

I sat for a long time, watching the birds and listening to the breeze rustling the leaves and the mountain stream gurgling over the shining rocks. In the distance, Mount Timpanogos majestically looked down on all that was happening in this mountain retreat, this refuge from the world, where big things can become small, making room for small things to become big.

# The Heavenly Grandstands
# Are Cheering

Have you ever set a goal and not reached it? The answer is probably yes. And how does that make you feel? Like somewhat of a failure? The answer again is probably yes. Then how do you avoid those feelings of failure that destroy your self-confidence? Just don't set any goals, right? Wrong! On the other hand, what happens when you have a goal clearly in your mind and you work and work and work until you reach your goal. How does that make you feel?

Six-year-old Kent sat at the breakfast table impatiently waiting for the family to gather for family prayer. This was quite irregular, since it had almost become a family ritual that everyone would be in places, kneeling by their chairs, when their mother called, "For the last time—if you don't come right now, you'll have to go without breakfast!" Kent's older sister smiled at that idle threat, which she had heard over the years. She hadn't remembered ever going without breakfast after such a threat, and she doubted that Kent would. Sometimes he would come slowly down the stairs; this would give him the feeling of being in control of the family while they waited for his grand entry. However, it was different this morning. He had gotten up early and prodded everyone to hurry.

Immediately following a breakfast of rolled oats (which he didn't like) and cinnamon toast (which he did like), Kent slipped away from the table while the family members reviewed their plans for the day, arranged for car-pool responsibilities, and determined who was to be where and when. Kent's plan was clear in his mind, and to delay was to postpone the realization of his goal.

He slipped out the door leading to the garage, apparently unnoticed, until the sound of the garage door gave him away. His mother left the table and hurried to the door, where she saw Kent struggling to get the bicycle between the car and the truck and out onto the driveway. "And where do you think you're going?" she asked. "I'm not *going* anywhere," he responded, pushing the bike out onto the driveway. His mother sensed his obvious determination. He had tried once before to ride the bike, but his legs were much too short, and it would require several months of growth before his goal could be accomplished.

"Maybe by the end of the summer," she had consoled him the last time he had tried to reach the pedals. That was only two weeks ago, and it was still the first part of June, with the whole summer ahead. The wait apparently made no sense to Kent, so his mother suggested that he push the bike up and down the street just to get the feeling of walking alongside it. Then she returned to the house and began her morning activities.

At about nine o'clock, she went to the front window to check on her son. He was steadying the bike and trying to get on. The bike wobbled back and forth, and before he had gone even a foot, it fell over with him on top, hitting his chin against the handlebar. His mother ran from the house, picked him up, brushed him off, examined his skinned chin, and offered to take the bike back to the garage for him. Kent wanted to keep it, and she agreed, assuming he would be content now to just push it after such a fall.

Before she could get back to the house, she heard a crash and turned to see the boy and his bike in a heap on the sidewalk. Again she ran to the rescue. This time she noticed blood coming from his elbow, which he had skinned. With such persistence from this child, Kent's mother determined that she should assist him in his efforts. She steadied the bike while he mounted and then ran alongside, holding it until he gained a little speed. He then called out, "Let go! Let go! I can do it by myself!"

Responding to his direction, she let go of the bike. He went only a few feet and, with the added speed this time, crashed again, hurting his knee. As he lay on the ground obviously injured, his mother regretted her decision to let go. Feeling responsible for this additional injury, she ran to his side, knelt down, and comforted him. "I'll take you in the house and we'll put lotion on your sores and give you a warm bath," she said. To this suggestion Kent sat upright and declared, "Mom, I don't want lotion on my sores and I don't want a warm bath. I want to learn to ride this bike."

He persisted throughout the day, with his mother holding the bike, running alongside, and then letting go briefly. When she had no more energy or time, she returned to the house thinking that he would surely have pursued his goal enough for one day.

Late in the afternoon Kent stood on the driveway and watched eagerly until he saw his father's truck coming down the street. When the truck was within a block from home, Kent began running. His father stopped to pick him up. "Dad," Kent cried, "I did it! I did it!" And so he did.

With his mother and father and some neighbors making up the audience for this great performance, Kent determinedly picked up his bicycle, pushed it over to the mailbox, and leaned it against the post while he mounted it. He made a quick survey to make sure all were watching, then pushed himself away from his support and tried to get both feet coordinated while the front wheel fishtailed back and forth like a leaf in the wind. He persisted until he had control enough to ride halfway down the block.

He had not yet learned to turn around or to stop, but that was not his goal for this day. He stopped by simply falling over as if he planned it that way. Then he got up and stood at his full height, proudly acknowledging the cheers from his supportive audience. "I did it all by myself, didn't I," he said, more as an announcement than a question.

After he got into bed that day, Kent still could not contain his joy. He jumped out of bed, ran to his parents' bedroom to use their phone, and dialed my telephone number. "Hello," I said. Without taking time to announce himself, he exploded with the exciting news. "I did it by myself, all by myself," he said. "What?" I asked. "What did you do?" "I rode the bike all by myself." "Oh, not really," I said, "not all by yourself," hoping to acknowledge the magnitude of his victory. "Yes, I did all by myself. I really did. Can you come and see?" "Tonight?" I asked. "Yes," he said, "right now." "I'm afraid it's too late tonight but I can come tomorrow." "In the morning?" he asked. "I'll be there at five o'clock tomorrow afternoon. Will that be all right?" I said. "Okay," he agreed. Then he added, "You'll be so proud of me."

That night I called Kent's mother and got the full details of his heroic accomplishment. I heard about the bruises, the determination, and the final victory.

And now, when I give thought to my goals, I remember what I learned from Kent. He awakened in the morning with the goal on his mind. Most likely he had envisioned himself riding that bike, just as the big boys do. When the vision of his accomplishment became clear enough, his confidence increased. In his mind he had already seen himself succeeding. With that kind of faith in himself, he knew he could do it. He didn't know how hard it would be, but he knew he could make it and that it would be worth the effort.

Next, he made a plan. Not a plan to sit and think about. Not a plan to wait until he was bigger or until others thought he was big enough. His plan was that right after breakfast—even before, if he had thought he could get away with it—he would get the bike and that very day he would accomplish his goal. His desire to ride would carry him through the hard and sometimes discouraging struggles. Such times always come with important goals, experiences that cause us to reach and stretch beyond where we are. Sometimes it's painful, and some person may give up and wait for another time, but with determination, regardless of the obstacles, most goals can be reached. Then we can say proudly to ourselves, "I did it! I did it!"

Self-mastery is deeply satisfying. It provides a tremendous source of confidence to tackle the next goal and the next and the next. And when a goal such as learning to ride a bike is a thing of the past, the lessons learned in the process can be called up and used again and again with each and every goal.

Sometimes there are friends and family to cheer us on. Other times there are those who would try to discourage us or say it can't be done. But whether a cheering crowd is visible or invisible, we can always remember that when we are striving for worthwhile goals, the "heavenly grandstands" are cheering. (Ezra Taft Benson, fourteen-stake fireside, Brigham Young University, March 4, 1979.)

# Knowledge

# The Treasures
# We Take with Us

Her lifelong dream had turned into what now seemed like a nightmare. During the long, hot summer days of picking potatoes and cucumbers, Alice had envisioned herself walking across the campus as a student at Brigham Young University. It was the goal that had kept her going when she would otherwise have given up.

Her determination had brought her to BYU for fall semester. And now the frustration, the pressure, the anguish that she faced seemed more like a nightmare than a reward for such effort. She hadn't planned it this way. In fact, after arriving she had hardly planned at all.

Alice was one of the students in my class. Somehow she hadn't realized the big difference between going to school and learning. She found the social side of college life more enticing than studying and learning. The urgency of preparing for her final exams hit her only after the opportunity for preparation had almost passed. It all seemed like a nightmare now. She must not fail, but she was unprepared. She had not committed herself to an education; she was just going to school.

She remembered people often asking her back home, "What do you want to be when you grow up?" Growing up had seemed so far away until this day. Now she was searching for the answer to that question, not for them but for herself. What did she want to do with her life and how did an education fit in?

We must all face that question eventually if we are to be responsible for our lives. When we find the answer, we have a sense of what we want to learn or what kind of job we may someday have or how we can become better mothers and wives, because of our education. We catch a glimpse of a bigger picture—a purpose, a destination, a course of action for this life that determines what we can become through the eternities. It's when we catch even a glimpse of the excitement, the benefits, the opportunities, the richness of life that an education can provide, that the discipline required to study becomes a small price to pay.

With an eye toward eternity, education is the treasure we will take with us and that will give us so much the advantage in the world to come. (See D&C 130:18–19.) And for today, it opens doors to opportunities that would otherwise be closed tight. Nephi wrote, "To be learned is good if they hearken unto the counsels of God." (2 Nephi 9:29.) If we lack wisdom we are to ask, and when we seek diligently we will know the truth. And the truth shall make us free (John 8:32)—free to make wise choices; free to experience life with ever-changing, wonderful, new horizons; free to speak up and speak out for what's right; free to influence those who are seeking truth; free to prepare in the time of youth for a rich and rewarding lifetime; free to hold on to the love of learning our whole life long, making every day more zestful.

Sister Camilla Kimball said, "What we must be concerned with is preparation for life, and that preparation is continuing education. Whether it is to earn a living or to rear a family, men and women both need to have the knowledge that enhances their natural talents." (Address at Spencer W. Kimball Tower dedication, Brigham Young University, March 9, 1982.) Preparation for life is for young women who marry and those who may never marry. It's for women who will have children to help educate and others who will not. It's for women who will need to support themselves and their children at some time in their lives.

For some of us, this may mean going to college or a trade school. To others, it may mean home study. To all of us, it means looking at the long-term goal of making education a lifelong process, not just a two- or four-year event after high school called "higher education."

One might ask, does pursuing an education contradict our goal to marry and have a family? Definitely not! We need to be educated for our families as well as ourselves. With all the contradictions and confusing voices, we are going to need our own clear direction more than ever before. A young woman should always keep the goal of marriage and family foremost in the choices she makes. But she must also be prepared for other rich and wonderful experiences in building the kingdom.

A woman who is now a mother of eleven children, dreamed in college of the lights of the stage, while taking classes in philosophy, economics, and political science and majoring in theater. Now she's on her own stage performing magnificently well. She has chosen to enrich, protect, and guard the home. This past summer she and another Mormon woman ran a campaign from their homes and were elected as two of four delegates to help choose a new leader for a political party. These same women later organized a rally in the city park on an issue they felt strongly would negatively affect life in their province in Canada.

I asked this sister how she manages to be so influential. "You have to know parliamentary procedure in public meetings," she replied. "If you do, you can safeguard democracy and your home by using the rules effectively."

"When and where does one learn these rules?" I asked.

She laughed and said, "Last night at supper, it went like this:

*Sarah: "Honorable chairman, the soup is good."*

*Chairman: "Can I have a motion to that effect?"*

*Sharon: "I move that we go on record stating the soup is good."*

*Chairman: "Could I have a second?" Seconded. "Any discussion?"*

*Amy: "It's too spicy."*

*Chairman: "We will proceed to vote."*

"The results of the dinner: The soup passed. The jam passed unanimously. And the motion in favor of the water was tabled for another time pending further investigation."

A mother who is well educated can help instill that same enthusiasm for learning in her children. Classes in home economics and child development and family relations can help strengthen our future families. And so can teaching and nursing, law and debate, political science, engineering, medicine, history, communications, and even statistics!

The question has been asked, if a woman is trained in such broad areas, will she be lured away from the home? In many ways, her education can strengthen her home. Down the road, higher education may give her more opportunity to be with her family, to set her own working hours, to have the know-how to go into business, to prepare her to meet the economic needs of her family if she must become the provider. Knowledge and intelligence are tools that can be used in righteousness or unrighteousness. Proper use can help us better protect and guard our homes.

Those who have a choice will be found protecting and guarding their families on the home front by the hearth. Others will be in foreign fields on occasion, working to keep the enemy away from our doors. Those fields may include participation in the PTA, in political parties, in civic organizations, and in various professions. Whether we are married or unmarried, with many children or none, education is important and is available right within the walls of our homes. No one needs to be deprived. We need to educate ourselves and prepare to defend our values and be a strong influence for righteousness.

When Queen Esther of the Old Testament was placed in the position to save the Jews in Persia from being put to death by appealing to her husband the king, her uncle Mordecai said to her, "Who knoweth whether thou art come to the kingdom for such a time as this?" (Esther 4:14.) Just as Esther was in the palace of the king to help her people, we each have important things to accomplish, many of them established before we came to this earth.

President George Q. Cannon wrote, "God has chosen us out of the world and has given us a great mission. I do not entertain a doubt myself but that we were selected and fore-ordained for the mission before the world was, that we had our parts allotted to us in this mortal state of existence as our Savior had His assigned to Him." (*Gospel Truth,* comp. Jerreld L. Newquist, Salt Lake City: Deseret Book, 1974, 1:22.).

As we seek to know the Lord's will and choose to carry it out, he will be there to guide us, to love us, to watch over us, to help us progress and learn. And because of our much learning, there will be many opportunities when our influence, our wisdom, our voice, and our vote will make the difference—not on whether the soup passes, but whether righteousness is defended.

What a young woman becomes when she grows up will be what she prepares for now.

*Knowledge*

# Seek Learning by
# Study and Faith

Many years ago, when I taught elementary school, I had a parent-teacher conference with the mother of one of my students. She expressed her deepest gratitude for a miracle that she felt had taken place. Her fourth-grade daughter was experiencing some learning difficulties and had struggled for months with the seemingly impossible task of mastering long division. But earlier that day she had come home in ecstasy, exclaiming, "Mom, I can do it!" Her mother thanked me for "saying it right," for "unlocking her little girl's mind," as she put it.

I didn't tell that mother that as a child I myself had mastered the art of figuring everything out the wrong way before I found the right way, and that I could therefore track her daughter's thought process. At that moment all of my own personal struggles with learning in years past seemed worth the effort. I thought of the admonition to "teach one another." (See D&C 88:77.) That day was a great payday for me as a teacher and as a person.

Each of us can be learning every day of our life. Time goes so fast that it makes fast learners of all of us—if we are seeking diligently. Through the Prophet Joseph Smith, the Lord counseled the Saints: "Seek ye diligently and teach one another words of wisdom; yea, seek ye out of the best books words of wisdom; seek learning, even by study and also by faith." (D&C 88:118.) If we can hold on to the thirst for knowledge during our whole life, every day will be more

93

zestful, and the speed with which we learn will not be nearly so important as *what* we learn.

President Joseph F. Smith wrote: "We hear concerning much of men who are specially gifted, of geniuses in the world's affairs; and many of us force ourselves to think that we are capable of little and therefore may as well take life easy since we do not belong to that favored class. True, not all are endowed with the same gifts, nor is everyone imbued with the strength of a giant; yet every son and daughter of God has received some talent and each will be held to strict account for the use or misuse to which it is put. The spirit of genius is the spirit of hard work." (*Juvenile Instructor* 18:689.)

I remember one time asking my father in anguish, "If the glory of God is intelligence and you are not smart, what will happen to you?" And my very wise and learned father, who never graduated from high school but who was self-taught and intelligent through diligent study and great faith, eased my concern when he explained, "My dear child, if you are diligent in your studies and do your very best and are obedient to God's commandments, one day, when you enter the holy temple, the university of the Lord, you will be prepared in your mind and spirit to learn and know all you need to know to return to your Father in heaven." It was faith in that promise that seemed to unlock my mind. It was study and faith working together.

But that was years ago, when spelling bees and times tables measured one's preparation for the future, at least for the next grade. What of today, with its computers, word processors, space travel, satellites, and newfound truth? Will we keep up? Should we? What learning should we seek? And what should we teach, write about, and talk about?

For each of us the challenges of today require the greatest preparation of mind, body, and spirit. Education presupposes the wide use of knowledge and should prepare people to develop the skills, attitudes, and values to build the kingdom of heaven here on earth. Our homes are a part of the kingdom. They should reflect some of the spiritual beauty of our celestial homeland, even when they are surrounded by storm clouds of darkness and are under attack.

The highest priority should always be to enrich, to protect, and to guard the home. To do this, we must have the Holy Spirit to guide us in our individual lives. We must know the truth and not be deceived. Our learning, our study, and our faith should be focused on that preparation which will strengthen the home and the family.

Our attitudes and decisions regarding learning are worthy of the most serious consideration. Wisdom is a gift of the Spirit. I am impressed by the apparent longing of Emma Smith, wife of the Prophet Joseph, for wisdom and understanding. When her husband decided to return to Carthage, a fateful decision that would lead to his death, she asked him to give her a blessing. He asked her to write the best blessing she desired, and he would sign it upon his return. Emma wrote the blessing, but the Prophet never returned from Carthage. Her words show that the greatest desire of her heart was for wisdom:

"First of all that I would crave, as the richest of heaven's blessings, would be wisdom from my Heavenly Father bestowed daily, so that whatever I might do or say, I could not look back at the close of the day with regret, nor neglect the performance of any act that would bring a blessing. I desire the Spirit of God to know and understand myself, that I might be able to overcome whatever of tradition or nature that would not tend to my exaltation in the eternal worlds. I desire a fruitful active mind, that I may be able to comprehend the designs of God, when revealed through His servants without doubting. I desire the spirit of discernment, which is one of the promised blessings of the Holy Ghost.

"I particularly desire wisdom to bring up all the children that are, or may be committed to my charge, in such a manner that they will be useful ornaments in the Kingdom of God, and in a coming day arise up and call me blessed.

"I desire prudence that I may not through ambition abuse my body and cause it to become prematurely old and care-worn, but that I may wear a cheerful countenance, live to perform all the work that I covenanted to perform in the spirit-world and be a blessing to all who may in any wise need aught at my hands.

"I desire with all my heart to honor and respect my husband as my head, ever to live in his confidence and by acting in unison with him retain the place which God has given me by his side. I desire to see that I may rejoice with [the daughters of Eve] in the blessings which God has in store for all who are willing to be obedient to His requirements. Finally, I desire that whatever may be my lot through

life I may be enabled to acknowledge the hand of God in all things."
(Relief Society Courses of Study 1985, p. 199.)

Everything we do takes time, and our time is our life. Some give
their life for little or nothing and then it is gone. But if our life is
spent in learning and teaching truth, used in righteousness, then the
investment is good. It is worth the price because the acquisition of
that knowledge is transportable. We are told that "whatever principle of intelligence we attain unto in this life, it will rise with us in
the resurrection. And if a person gains more knowledge and intelligence through his diligence and obedience than another, he will
have so much the advantage in the world to come." (D&C 130:
18–19.)

We are in an era of knowledge that has been termed an information explosion. Much of the learning of the world quickly becomes
obsolete; much of what we learned last year is now outdated. In
contrast, gospel knowledge is never outdated; it is gospel truth.

My heart aches and I am troubled when I hear of people who
spend much of their time watching a distorted portrayal of life day
after day on television soap operas, or who view mundane video
programs or read books with similar content, in exchange for
actively participating in this life and preparing for the life to come. If
we were to spend most of our time on the trivia of life, what would
be the quality of our reservoir of learning? How deep the water?
What would its color be? What could we draw up in time of need?
What could we recall from the depth of memory?

President Joseph F. Smith wrote this about learning and our
ability to recall: "In reality a man cannot forget anything. He may
have a lapse of memory; he may not be able to recall at the moment
a thing that he knows, or words that he has spoken; he may not have
the power at his will to call up these events and words; but let God
Almighty touch the mainspring of the memory, and awaken recollection, and you will find then that you have not even forgotten a
single idle word that you have spoken!" (Improvement Era 6:503–4.)

One day we will recall all things that have come through our
minds, and this could be a magnificent and glorious blessing.
Imagine having quick access to a reservoir of knowledge accumulated over an entire lifetime, all of it available for immediate recall.
All of the good things stored there that have been just out of

reach, forgotten for a time, will still be part of our learning. The frustrations of forgetting will be a thing of the past.

The question is: What will we have to call up from the books we have read, the TV we have watched, the videos we have viewed? What are the things to which we have given our ear or attention or our life?

Elder John A. Widtsoe helps us understand more clearly our responsibilities for what we need to learn: "We need, in this Church and Kingdom, for our own and the world's welfare a group of men and women in their individual lives who shall be as a light to the nations, and really standards for the world to follow. Such a people must be different from the world as it now is . . . unless the world has the same aim that we have. We are here to build Zion to Almighty God, for the blessing of all the world. In that aim we are unique and different from all other peoples. We must respect that obligation, and not be afraid of it. We cannot walk as other men, or talk as other men, or do as other men, for we have a different destiny, obligation, and responsibility placed upon us, and we must fit ourselves for that great destiny and obligation." (*Conference Report,* April 1940, p. 36.)

In other words, you can't be a life saver if you look like all the other swimmers on the beach.

What is the path, the way, for seeking learning? By study? Yes, but also by faith. The voice of the Spirit teaches truth. One young man, just nineteen years old and in his second week at the Missionary Training Center, explained how this works: "When you study with the Spirit, it is incredible how fast you learn. One time in particular, when I was working very hard and felt the Spirit strongly, I learned an entire concept in a little over five minutes. I'm beginning to get a sense of the power that is behind this work."

It is our responsibility to seek learning by study and by faith in order that we might fulfill our covenant to stand as witnesses and to build the faith of others. We are surrounded by the Korihors of our day just as Alma faced them in his day—those who refer to the "foolish" traditions of our fathers, those who would raise questions, distort the truth, confuse us, demand a sign and seek to raise doubts in our minds, even some who profess membership in the Church. As these questioners surround our camp and threaten our safety, our testimonies must ring strong and true, unwavering and uncompromising. In addition, "a testimony is not enough," President J. Reuben Clark warned. "You must have besides this, one of the rarest and most precious of all the many elements of human character,—moral courage."

While an inquiring mind is most desirable, the tendency for some is to be forever testing even the ordinary events in life to see if they are valid. There are some things that have to be accepted in faith at least for the moment, and perhaps the questions will be put on the shelf to be answered at a later time. To constantly peck away at even the most basic gospel principles can eventually destroy, at least for ourselves—and sometimes for others—everything that is important. Sometimes our desire to test everything may not be so much the result of lack of confidence in the truth as it is the lack of security within ourselves. We need never fear truth when it is used in righteousness.

President Joseph F. Smith gives us this enlightening observation: "The mere stuffing of the mind with a knowledge of facts is not education. The mind must not only possess a knowledge of truth, but the soul must revere it, cherish it, love it as a priceless gem; and this human life must be guided and shaped by it in order to fulfil its destiny. The mind should not only be charged with intelligence, but the soul should be filled with admiration and desire for pure intelligence which comes of a knowledge of the truth. The truth can only make him free who hath it, and will continue in it. And the word of God is truth, and it will endure forever. Educate yourself not only for time, but also for eternity." (*The Contributor* 16:570.)

We must not be casual in our commitment to academic excellence. We must row with both oars—study and faith—if we are to be fully prepared and reach our goal. We are not immune in the Church today from those who are pulling only on the intellectual oar. Without balance in our effort, we will find ourselves going in circles.

If a person chooses to set aside the things of the Spirit while pursuing only academic endeavors, the outcome is predictable. For those who choose to row with only one oar for an extended period of time, one set of muscles is strengthened while the others become atrophied. At a later date, as graduates with degrees, such individuals may stack their acquired academic knowledge against the thin threads of a faith that has been weakened through neglect. Their spiritual strength may have remained at or retrogressed to an elementary school level. And when they endeavor to make judgments of things of the Spirit that come only by faith, the great reservoir of truth into which they could have dipped will be shallow, discolored, or stagnant. This is the condition of which Nephi spoke:

"O that cunning plan of the evil one! O the vainness, and the frailties, and the foolishness of men! When they are learned they think they are wise, and they hearken not unto the counsel of God, for they set it aside, supposing they know of themselves, wherefore, their wisdom is foolishness and it profiteth them not. And they shall perish. But to be learned is good if they hearken unto the counsels of God." (2 Nephi 9:28–29.)

It is sad to realize that some Latter-day Saints blessed with great intellectual capacity are depriving themselves by using only one oar. Hence the wise counsel to "seek learning by study and also by faith," which helps ensure that we stay on course.

There is much that we can learn by study, but truth cannot be acquired by study alone. We must seek learning by faith also, if we are ever to know for ourselves that God the Father lives; that Jesus Christ is his divine Son; that they appeared personally to the young Joseph Smith; that through Joseph the "only true and living church upon the face of the whole earth" (D&C 1:30) was restored. It is by faith that we can know that Joseph Smith and his successors are prophets, seers, and revelators; that they receive direct revelation concerning the administration of the Church; and that the Book of Mormon was in fact translated by the Prophet through the power of God.

Many insights to learning by faith were given during the Savior's ministry. At one time during the Feast of the Passover he went into the temple and taught, and "the people listened intently. The Jewish teachers were amazed, so much so that they questioned among themselves, 'How knoweth this man letters, having never learned?' Jesus was not a graduate of their schools of the rabbis. They had their training by tradition passed from one great rabbinical teacher to another and claiming to reach back to Moses. But where had this tradesman, this uneducated Galilean, learned?

"Jesus answered their troubled questions saying, 'My doctrine is not mine, but his that sent me.' Then, knowing they would dispute it, he offered this test: 'If any man will do his will, he shall know of the doctrine, whether it be of God, or whether I speak of myself.' The burden of proof was placed on the listeners. It was an invitation as well. Try the doctrine; introduce it into your very being. Live it and you will know." (Ardeth G. Kapp and Judith S. Smith, *The Light and the Life,* Bookcraft, 1985, pp. 71–72.)

The Pharisees of the Savior's day kept watch, hoping to find any reason to question his message. They had trained their eyes and ears to see and hear what they hoped was wrong—whether it was healing on the Sabbath or winnowing the wheat or forgiving the woman in sin. They knew the law; they had studied the law. Each time Jesus' message was heard, there was fervor among them as they counseled together to determine if there were weaknesses or errors in his message to prove that he was not the Son of God. The choice of their course closed their ears and hearts and dulled their spirits so they could not hear the message. While they haggled over words and details looking for fault, they missed the message they might have learned by the Spirit and by faith that would have saved their eternal lives. They were "ever learning, and never able to come to the knowledge of the truth." (2 Timothy 3:7.)

This was not the case with the two thousand stripling sons of Helaman, who fought with miraculous faith and none were slain: "They had never fought, yet they did not fear death; and they did think more upon the liberty of their fathers than they did upon their lives; yea, they had been taught by their mothers, that if they did not doubt, God would deliver them. And they rehearsed . . . the words of their mothers, saying: We do not doubt our mothers knew it." (Alma 56:47–48.)

It is my testimony that if we continue to seek learning by study and by faith, we will receive the truth as the Spirit bears witness, and the power of discernment will be ours to guide us and protect us from being deceived. We have been promised that as we study diligently, we shall learn of Him; and as we seek diligently, we shall surely find Him.

*Knowledge*

# The Irrigation
# Ditch

The alfalfa patch was best of all, partly because it was located at the lower edge of our eighty acres by the grove of elm trees, and partly because of the irrigation ditch, its banks covered with yellow buffalo beans, which marked the boundary along the south side of our fields. But mostly, I think, it was best of all because of the smell. It is the recollection of that smell of alfalfa in the stillness of the early morning that brings every emotion of that occasion back over the years as clearly as though I were experiencing it for the first time. In the early morning, before breakfast, when one is fresh from sleep, the smell is the very best.

Dad and I would often walk together through our fields. He'd wear high rubber boots and carry a shovel over his shoulder, a long stem of wheat hanging from the corner of his mouth. I loved the way the heavy morning dew, still sparkling like crystals on the alfalfa leaves, made our boots appear new and shiny with each step. As I walked by his side, occasionally he'd stop and pick up a handful of earth, almost reverently, then let it slip through his fingers as the breeze carried it gently to the ground. Looking upward into the cloudless blue sky, he'd say, "God has given us this good earth, but we must do our part," and then almost under his breath he'd repeat, "We must do our part." It always seemed as if he were talking to someone but not to me, so I didn't feel the need to respond.

On this particular morning we walked together through the alfalfa until we stood side by side at the edge of the main irrigation ditch. We had not come this way before, and I didn't know the plan, but I had learned to watch and listen first and save questions for later.

Dad took the shovel from his shoulder and made his way down the bank of the ditch to the water's edge. Then he turned and, with one foot high on the bank, stretched his big hand toward me. Taking my hand in his, he steadied me until we stood together near the water. I could often tell by the shape of his eyes and the angle of his chin the nature of the lesson he was about to teach, and I knew this was going to be "a good learning opportunity," as he always called it, quietly adding, "if your attitude is right."

"We're going to vault across the ditch," he explained. "I'll show you how."

I watched him as he reached with the shovel to about the middle of the ditch. He poked several times to avoid the rocks before he pushed the shovel deep into the bottom. Then, pulling the handle at an angle toward him, he took hold with both hands and swung forward, landing on the other side. "Like that," he said.

I watched carefully. I had one more chance to observe before it was my turn. He demonstrated again, returning to my side of the ditch.

Now was the time for the questions. "Dad, what if I don't make it?" And he always saved his counsel to use when it counted. "If you give it all you've got, you'll make it." Then I noticed a slight smile as he further counseled, "And if you don't, you'll land in the middle and get soaked."

"And then what will I do?" was my next question.

"You'll still have to get to the other side."

With those options, it seemed important to try hard to follow his first counsel. Dad didn't rush me. It was as though he knew the crossing of the ditch was perhaps even more important than the water in the ditch he used for irrigating.

I stood and watched. Suddenly there seemed to be a vast audience encouraging me. The birds in the elm trees nearby were chirping, almost as though they were cheering. A big bumblebee that had been weaving back and forth among the yellow buffalo beans along the bank even joined in by buzzing in a circle while casting a shadow on the water's surface for water skeeters to dodge.

As I stood for some time watching those skeeters skim the

surface of the water, Dad offered his next suggestion. "Honey, don't concentrate on the water. You have to keep your eye on the bank on the other side. It's keeping your eye on the target that makes all the difference."

I guess he sensed my readiness and also the proper timing. He slowly pulled the smooth handle of the shovel toward me and helped me get a firm hold with both hands. I looked up and noticed his straw hat hiding his wavy hair, his eyebrows forming a partial frame for the kind blue eyes that could look right through you. He smiled and said, "Give it all you've got."

With that, my hands tightened on the handle of the shovel. I paused a moment and then fixed my eyes on a particular clump of buffalo beans on the other side of the ditch. Taking a deep breath, I tightened my grip, glanced quickly at Dad, gave it all I had, and swung forward. I made it, landing right on top of the buffalo beans.

Quickly I turned to look back at Dad. He gave his usual sign for victory by clasping both hands together raising them above his head, and shouting as though it were a glorious accomplishment. "I knew you could do it!" I watched then as he jumped the ditch with such ease that I wondered, Why all the fuss just for me?

It was a good morning, and by early afternoon we had cleared all the small ditches of any grass or weeds that might obstruct the free flow of the precious water. Dad paused now and pulled out his pocket watch, which was tied to his belt loop with an old shoelace. With a quick glance at his watch and then a look up at the sun, as if to check either his watch or the sun, I was never sure which, he announced, "Time for lunch."

We headed for the trees near the old granary. It was a familiar place. A narrow path had been worn through the grass leading toward the trees. In the middle of the trees, the tall grass lay flattened from many previous lunches. I sat down in a favorite spot, and Dad separated the tall grass where our lunch pail had been placed to keep it cool. With the lunch pail opened, he removed his straw hat, the imprint of the inside band still on his forehead, and wiped his damp brow with one big sweeping motion of his arm. After a brief expression of thanks for the bounties of life, we were ready to eat.

It was the big water jug covered with wet burlap that I remember best. Something about the smell, that wet coarse texture so close to my nose, and tipping my head back waiting for the clear, cool water to touch my lips while Dad held the jug, made the whole event seem almost like a ritual. After I had my turn, Dad took his.

Following lunch, we stretched out on the soft, tall grass and looked up through the trees. Sometimes I'd talk and Dad would listen, or Dad would talk and I would listen. As I recall it now, it seems as if Dad always listened as much as he talked, but this time it was my turn to listen.

"You know, Ardie," he said, "you learned an important lesson today."

I quickly agreed. "Yes, I learned to jump the ditch."

"Yes, you did," he said. Then he raised up on one elbow and asked, "Just how do you think you did that?"

That sounded like a strange question to me since he saw how I did it, but he seemed to want more, so I tried to explain. "Well, first I watched you, and then when it was my turn, I got a scary feeling inside."

That seemed to be the thing that he was after as he quickly inquired, "And then what?"

"Well, I just looked at the buffalo beans on the other side and tried real hard and jumped across."

As if to reinforce the lesson, he reviewed it again. "That's exactly right, Ardie. You had your eye on the other side and gave it all you had, and you made it."

Moving the support of his arm, he lay back on the grass and we watched in silence as the feathery clouds began to invade the blue sky. We could hear the birds in the trees, the distant moo of the cows, and the faint sound of the water falling over the drop in the ditch.

It seemed like quite a while until Dad spoke again, and then in a tone that remains with me yet. "Ardie, my dear," he said, "there are a lot of irrigation ditches to cross in life. Many of them you must cross alone." Then, as a final summary to his lesson, he repeated, "Keep your eye on the other side, give it all you've got, and you'll make it."

# Choice
## and
# Accountability

# What Have You
# to Declare?

It was the last day of the school quarter, and finals were over. With a group of fellow students, I piled into a friend's old car for the trip home to Canada. There were always more people than comfort would allow, but what we lost in comfort, we saved in cost. With tuna sandwiches and whatever else we could find in the cupboard, we headed north.

At the border we were required to open our suitcases—usually full of gray-white laundry that we hoped our mothers could remedy. The customs officer stirred around and routinely asked, "What have you to declare?" Wise travelers usually make a list of the valuables they are carrying to facilitate the passage through customs and expedite their arrival home. For us, there was never much to declare—just our name, our destination, and our present place of residence.

As we crossed the border, I began wondering about our ultimate journey, our journey to our eternal home. When we reach that border crossing, how will we respond to the question, "What have you to declare?" I believe that the list we will each be required to present will be written "not with ink," as Paul said, "but with the Spirit of the Living God; not in tables of stone, but in fleshy tables of the heart." (2 Corinthians 3:3.) I believe it will be the evidence of our love for each other that will qualify us for the passage. And the customs officer—who will that be? Nephi tells us what we might expect: "Behold, the way for man is narrow, but it lieth in a straight course before him, and the keeper of the gate is the Holy One of Israel; and he employeth no servant there; and there is none other way save it be by the gate; for he cannot be deceived, for the Lord God is his name." (2 Nephi 9:41.)

As I, in my times of quiet meditation, consider the ecstasy and joy of experiences we have in this life, I believe they will be paled by what we will experience in that moment when we give an accounting to the Holy One of Israel, a silent declaration of accountability that will speak loudly of how we exercised our agency, of the choices we made, and, finally, of the values and principles we claimed as our very own to protect us and direct us over the treacherous narrow passages on our journey.

I know something about the risk of traveling over icy winter roads when travel warnings are posted, when the danger of blizzards threatens our safety and sometimes delays our progress while loved ones take turns standing watch, waiting for us. I knew in those days that family prayers had been offered in our behalf that we might return home safely.

Can you, in your own thoughts, sense that moment of greeting, even if you haven't had such an experience? On the other hand, consider the tragedy if the highway patrol had to report to anxious loved ones that the mountain pass and highway were steep and slick, that you must not have read the warning signs or were sleepy and not alert enough to respond to the dangers, that you had missed the turn—and no one survived. Think of those loved ones waiting. I want to share with you what I believe will be the joy as we approach our heavenly home. But first, let us consider what road signs we are following to secure our safe travel.

Would you knock on the door of your own soul and inquire within concerning the markers or values you declare publicly and privately, the ones you have determined to follow. If we use only external markers, such as other people's values or rules, regulations or policies, if we use only external signals to determine our course, what will happen on a stormy night when the clouds and fog obscure the signals and we are alone in the dark? It isn't a committee or an institution or a crew that sets our sail. We must have our own clearly defined values burning brightly within. Only then will we have an inner court to which we can appeal for judgment of our performance—*our* performance, not someone else's.

I find myself reaching and stretching when I learn of others who navigate well in troubled waters. Even more heroic is the conduct of those who make choices in waters that appear to be calm and of little concern to others. Let me illustrate with this account:

"I was driving to a scene I didn't want to see. A man had accidentally backed his pickup truck over his baby granddaughter in the driveway of the family home. It was a fatality.

"As I parked, I saw a stocky white-haired man in cotton work-clothes standing near a pickup. Cameras were trained on him and reporters were sticking microphones in his face. Looking totally bewildered, he was trying to answer their questions. Mostly he was only moving his lips, blinking and choking up. I can still see in my mind's eye that devastated old man, looking down at a place in the driveway where the child had been.

"Beside the house was a freshly spaded flowerbed and nearby a pile of dark rich earth. 'I was just backing up there to spread that good dirt,' he said to me, though I had not asked him anything. 'I didn't even know she was outdoors.'

"I went into the house to find someone who would provide a recent photo of the toddler. A few minutes later, with all the details in my notebook and a studio photo of the child in my pocket, I went into the kitchen where the police had said the body was. Entering the kitchen, I came upon this scene:

"On a Formica-topped table, backlighted by a frilled curtain window, lay the tiny body wrapped in a clean white sheet. The grandfather had managed to stay away from the crowd and was sitting on a chair beside the table in profile to me and unaware of my presence, looking uncomprehendingly at the swaddled corpse. The house was very quiet. A clock ticked. As I watched, the grandfather slowly leaned forward. He curved his arms like parentheses around the head and feet of the little form, then pressed his face to the shroud and remained motionless.

"In that hushed moment I recognized the markings of a prize-winning news photograph. I appraised the light, adjusted the lens, locked a bulb in the flash gun, raised the camera, and composed the scene in the viewfinder. Every element of the picture was perfect—the grandfather, in his plain clothes, his white hair backlighted by sunlight, the child's form wrapped in the sheet, the atmosphere of the simple home. Outside the police could be seen inspecting the pickup while the child's mother and father leaned into each other's arms.

"I don't know how many seconds I stood there unable to snap that shutter. I was keenly aware of the powerful story-telling value that photo would have and my professional conscience told me to take it. Yet I couldn't make my hand fire that flashbulb and intrude on the poor man's island of grief. At length, I lowered the camera and crept away, shaking with doubt about my suitability for the journalistic profession.

"I never told the city editor or any fellow reporters about that missed opportunity for a perfect news picture. Every day on the newscasts and the papers, we see pictures of people in extreme conditions of grief and despair. Human suffering has become a spectator sport, and sometimes when I am watching the news film, I remember that day. I still feel right about what I did." (James Alexander Thom, "The Perfect Picture.")

As we look back to yesterday, last week, last year, the question for each of us is, Do I feel right about what I did? As we travel the treacherous way of mortal life, we kick up dust in our daily living. We make mistakes, but in quiet moments of meditation, when the dust settles and we examine our thoughts and actions to carefully and honestly determine what it is that we have to declare, we all need to make continuous "inflight correction."

I like what C. S. Lewis says about that process: "A wrong sum can be put right: but only by going back till you find the error and work it afresh from that point." And who determines if it is an error? The regulations and policy officers? Yes, if they must, but hopefully not. To them, it may not even be seen as an error. But that may not excuse us in our own minds.

In the novel *The Chosen,* by Chaim Potok, the Jewish father cries out to the master of the universe as he addresses him in prayer in behalf of his son, who has a brilliant and capable mind. The father says, "A mind like this I need for a son? A heart I need for a son. A soul I need for a son. Compassion I want from my son, righteousness, mercy, strength to suffer and carry pain. That I want from my son. Not a mind without a soul." The son, speaking of his father, says, "He taught me to look inside myself, to find my own strength, to walk around inside myself in company with my soul."

When you walk around inside yourself and find your own

strength and live in company with your own soul, can you answer the questions the way you would like to? Would you have snapped the shutter on the camera in that private moment? When we get a wrong sum, can we put it right? In a public setting, would there ever be a chance that we would succumb to the pressures of power or prestige or position or popularity?

Our values, our road signs that keep us on course and on schedule, are not to be tucked away for safekeeping. They are to be carried daily, used continuously, tested against our performance regularly, and literally worn out as a constant measuring device that keeps us accountable. The powers and plans of Satan are cunning and subtle and very real. The most destructive threats of our day are not nuclear war, not famine, not economic disaster. Rather, they are the despair, the discouragement, the despondency, the defeat caused by the discrepancy between what we believe to be right and how we live our lives. We are on a stormy sea. These are threatening times, and we may be ignoring or even cutting ourselves loose from the very signals that would save us.

May I tell you about another time I crossed that border between the United States and Canada, this time with family members. We were taking our parents back home, knowing that for Dad it would be the last time. As we cleared customs, Dad raised up from his sickbed in the back of the car and commented, "This prairie has never looked so beautiful. It's at its very best for my last inspection."

During our brief stay in our old hometown, we sauntered down the gravel road past the tall cottonwood trees, where the old school had stood. Dad took the lead. "It was the old bell," he said, and we all looked in the same direction, seeing it clearly in our mind's eye. "The school bell kept us in line. There were two bells," he went on. "A fifteen-minute bell would ring six times, giving ample warning before the final five-minute bell sounded a simple dingdong—and you'd better be there." His weakened voice increased in intensity as he added, "It's important to listen for the bell."

As we mused together in silence for a time, I pondered the possibility of my own inner bell being silenced, if only for a moment. As if reading my thoughts, Dad lay back on the soft, grassy ditch where we had stopped and began with a familiar phrase we had all learned to love. "I remember the story in the old fourth-grade reader," he said. He began his story.

"There was an old and very large inch-cape rock. It got its name from being located just one inch below the water's surface, where it couldn't be seen, and it lay dangerously in the path of the mariners returning from sea. Many seamen had lost their ships and their lives because of the rock, especially in times of storm. An abbot in the small seashore town of Aberbrothok devised a solution to this life-threatening hazard. With great care and in the face of considerable danger, he fastened a buoy with a large bell on the inch-cape rock. From then on the bell rang continuously and faithfully with the motion of the waves of the sea.

"Ralph the Rover was a bit of a pirate and he disliked the praises the abbot received from the mariners whose lives he spared. So one day, Ralph the Rover cut the bell from the inch-cape rock.

> *Down sank the bell with a gurgling sound,*
> *The bubbles rose and burst around,*
> *Quoth Sir Ralph, "The next who comes to the rock,*
> *Won't bless the abbot of Aberbrothok."*
> *Sir Ralph the Rover sailed away,*
> *He scoured the seas for many a day.*

"On his way back, it was night and the sea was high, and he thought the moon would be up. In the darkness, he said with great anxiety—but only to himself—'I wish I could hear the bell of the inch-cape rock,' and the rhyme continued:

> *Sir Ralph the Rover tore his hair,*
> *He cursed himself in deep despair.*
> *The waves rushed in on every side,*
> *The ship sinking beneath the tide."*
> (Robert Southey, *The Inch Cape Rock*)

Dad's stories always stood without any editorializing, left for me to figure out the message. I am not sure how I felt then, but in years since, I have come to feel that rather than wishing to silence the bell within, I feel myself strain a little so that I might hear it more clearly.

After our trip to Canada, Dad and I talked about going home on that final journey and about the border crossing. His body was now less than one hundred pounds, and his mortal journey was coming to a close. He talked about the sweetness and sacredness of these times and spoke of the nearness of the Lord, the Holy One of Israel, the gatekeeper. Life had presented ample and enough struggles, and he had used them to prove himself worthy and to cleanse the soul. And he was ready for the border crossing.

That last day, Dad spoke of Addison, his younger brother who had gone on before him. I wondered if his brother, and maybe his mother and father, were standing at the kitchen window an hour before his expected arrival, anxious for his safe return home.

By midafternoon I had decided to sit with Dad. His eyes seemed to be open, yet he wasn't seeing me. I took his hand in mine, a hand that had spanked me and blessed me and caressed me throughout my life. "Dad," I whispered. He didn't respond. "If you know I'm here, please squeeze my hand." I wasn't sure if there was a squeeze, but it didn't seem like it. I bent over and put my cheek next to his very bony cheek, with my hand on the other side of his face. I waited just a second, then straightened up. He looked at me just a moment, and in his eyes I saw complete peace—joy, trust, confidence, and anticipation, all mingled together in that look. He was ready for the border crossing and the gatekeeper, the Holy One of Israel. A tear escaped the corner of his eye, and I pressed my cheek to his again. There are things we cannot find words or even sounds to express, but in that moment I had some sense of what that final crossing might be and the ecstasy that we'll never fully understand in this life.

Someday we too will arrive at a border crossing and will have an opportunity to make a declaration. We will remember then that we were free "to choose liberty and eternal life, through the great Mediator of all men, or to choose captivity and death, according to the captivity and power of the devil; for he seeketh that all men might be miserable like unto himself." (2 Nephi 2:27.) The choices we make each day of our lives will make us what we are at that time. When we open our luggage on our final journey and make our declaration, will we be carrying gray-white laundry as evidence of the unwise choices we have made along the way? There will be for each of us many unwise choices, but when we do our part, a cleansing will have taken place, and we will not be ashamed but will be so very, very grateful.

Alma's teaching explains it for us: "There can no man be saved except his garments are washed white; yea, his garments must be purified until they are cleansed from all stain, through the blood of him of whom it has been spoken by our fathers, who should come to redeem his people from their sins." (Alma 5:21.) We are God's children, you and I. He is our Father, and he loves us very much. He wants us to come home, to his home—our home after the completion of our time here. I know that he guides us and comforts us and forgives us; that he hears our knock and waits at the gate for our return. And to the question, "What have you to declare?" it will be written in the fleshy table of our heart, our journey at a glance. May we stand in confidence as evidence of our faith in the Lord Jesus Christ, our daily repentance, living true to the ordinances and covenants that qualify us for the companionship of the Holy Ghost and prepare us to stand as a witness of Christ at all times.

# The Rescue

She had come to my door many times during the past few years, sometimes when she had skipped a class at school and other times late at night. We spent hours talking about how things were with her. "It all started in the sixth grade," she explained one day when she spoke of her dislike for school, her parents, and the Church. "I knew my parents wouldn't approve of some of the things I was doing, so I kept everything a secret. I refused to talk to them. I guess that was the real beginning. I began doing a lot of things I shouldn't, and I quit talking to my parents. I wish now I could go back," she added, "but how do you go back?"

For several years many people had tried to get through to Mindy, but it was as though the lines of communication were down. No messages could get through. Occasionally her mother would call me and ask anxiously if I saw any signs that might give any hope of Mindy's attitude changing. "It is so unlike her," her mother would always explain. "She was such an obedient happy child, I can't understand what has happened or what we have done wrong. I'd do anything to help her, but she won't listen to a thing we say."

Mindy often complained, "My parents won't listen to me. They're too busy. They don't like my music, they don't like my clothes, they don't like my friends, and they don't like me." Any attempt to talk things over at home resulted in shouting, crying, and anger. "It's my life!" she exclaimed. "It's no one else's business what I do with my life—I can take care of myself!"

Mindy's Young Women adviser at church was determined to reach her, to include her in the class activities and help her be part of the group. The girls in her Young Women class worked together to make her a quilt for her birthday. That would surely help her know they cared about her. They worked hard to include her in their group, but whenever they called her on the phone she wasn't home, and she would never call back even though her mother gave her the message.

When her mother told her the girls at church had invited her to a class party, her response was the same. "I'm not going to that party," she said, not knowing that it was a party to celebrate her birthday. The party was being held at the adviser's home. Some of the girls in the class had offered to pick Mindy up, but she refused their offer. Her adviser, knowing where she might be, left the party, drove around a few blocks, and saw her walking down the hill toward the mall. She drove up alongside her and called, "Mindy! Mindy!" Mindy turned her head and began running in the other direction. Her adviser could not get through to her. There seemed no way to communicate with her. Mindy had found new friends where the lights were dim, the music loud, and the world enticing. *Why trade that for the things they do at church?* she thought. She had no fear. It was a new way of life and very exciting.

The bishop inquired about Mindy. He wanted to visit with her, help her, and encourage her, but she refused to meet with him. This may be because there was no way to hide the strong smell of tobacco that was always present wherever she was.

At school the counselor called Mindy in for an interview. She had received a report indicating that Mindy's academic and attendance records were poor. Finally the school officials determined that Mindy could no longer participate in regular school activities, and they referred her to an alternate school that dealt with students who had special problems. A teacher was assigned to visit her once a week to help with her lessons, but Mindy had no interest in lessons and she wouldn't listen to the teacher.

Mindy was in trouble, and no one could reach her. She lived in a world of her own making. Loud music, videos, and her newfound friends helped isolate her from those who would have come to her rescue if given a chance, but she could not—or would not—listen to their warnings. She was in danger, and no one was getting through. She was in deep water.

So it is with each of us as we meet the challenges of life. It is our maiden voyage, a new experience, and we are inexperienced travelers in a strange land.

And so it was with another voyage that ended in disaster. The great White Star ocean liner *Titanic,* the largest ship the world had ever known, sailed on her maiden voyage from England to New York on April 10, 1912. This great ship, which was thought to be unsinkable, carried more than 2200 passengers. On Sunday morning, April 14, the steamer *Caronia* sent a message to the captain of the *Titanic:* "Captain, Titanic—Westbound steamers report bergs, growlers and field ice in 42 degrees N. from 49 degrees to 51 degrees W." The message was acknowledged but not acted upon.

Just before noon another ship in the area, the *Baltic,* also warned the *Titanic* of the ice. The captain read the message, then handed it to one of his officers, who stuffed it in his pocket.

Later in the day a third ocean liner, the *Californian,* sent a message about icebergs but no one bothered to take it down. By ten that evening at least seven messages warning of ice had been sent, but those who could have changed the course away from the danger chose not to listen. To one message, the *Titanic* responded, "Shut up, shut up; keep out. I am talking to Cape Race; you are jamming my signals." The man on duty had been warned to watch for icebergs, but nothing unusual appeared as the *Titanic* raced across the calm, black sea.

Suddenly in the blackness of the night, the lookout reported a small dark object that grew larger and closer. The man rang the warning bell three times and called the bridge on the phone to report the danger. "What do you see?" asked a calm voice at the other end. "Iceberg right ahead" was the reply. "Thank you," came the response. Nothing more was said.

Suddenly the foaming green sea water exploded through the *Titanic's* side. The conclusion was inescapable. The *Titanic* was sinking. Within ninety minutes she would rest on the bottom of the ocean floor, 13,000 feet below.

"Send the call for assistance," the captain ordered.

The officials on the ill-fated *Titanic* tried desperately to get through to the *Californian,* who had tried to call a warning earlier. But the *Californian* communication lines had closed down at 11:30. The ship was less than ten miles from the sinking liner, but there was no way to get through. Another ship some distance away, the *Carpathia,* picked up the SOS signal: "Come at once. We have struck a berg." The answer came back, "We are coming as quickly as possible and expect to be there within four hours." The *Carpathia* was a 14-knot ship, but that night for three and a half hours she worked up to 17 knots.

The passengers on the *Titanic* had no fear. They were unaware of the danger they were in. When instructed to get into the few lifeboats available, they wondered if it was a boat drill. Why trade the bright decks of the *Titanic* for a few dark hours in a rowboat? they asked. "We are safer here than in that little boat," one man said. The band was playing ragtime, the best band on the Atlantic. Why leave the lights, the music, and the excitement?

At 12:45 A.M., a rocket shot into the air. Immediately everyone on the deck knew what that meant. There was no time for lights or music; there was hardly time to say good-bye. The *Titanic*'s stern steadily lifted, and suddenly her lights snapped off. They came on again only briefly, then went out forever. As the largest ship the world had ever known sank out of sight, the sea closed over the flagstaff of her stern and she was gone.

The *Carpathia* never slackened her speed in an effort to come to the rescue. At 3:35 A.M. she was almost there. In the distance the crew saw a green light from a small boat. Reaching the boat, the officer called out, "Where is the *Titanic?*" "Gone," was the reply. "She sank at 2:20 A.M." "Were there any people left on board?" "Hundreds, perhaps thousands," was the response.

At a youth conference I saw a young woman showing signs of approaching an iceberg. She was getting into deep water. Her dress, her conduct, her language, and her behavior indicated she was not hearing the warnings—those guidelines that often appear more like harsh rules than wise warnings. It was her adviser who pleaded with me. "Maybe she will listen to you," she said. "I've tried and tried." Any possibility was worth the effort, so I agreed. If the young woman and her adviser would come together, I would be happy to spend some time with them. We sat on the steps behind the stage, away from the activities, and I told them about a great and powerful ship on her maiden voyage, the *Titanic*.

It wasn't a time for judgment or preaching, but one more attempt to break through lines that had been closed down for a time. We talked about the communication lines we use in prayer and how our Father in heaven is always on duty and will never close down the lines. Our prayers can always be heard, and the message can get through.

We talked about the still, small voice, the warning signals, and the danger of icebergs on our journey home. In our time together, I saw and felt the love and concern of an adviser who, with the help of the Lord, was reaching out to a young woman in trouble. Tears filled the eyes of the young girl, for she could not deny the love of her adviser for her.

As we met together, the adviser prayed—she gave the call for help. She talked to Heavenly Father about her love for her young friend and her great desire to help this young woman build a good relationship with her parents. She spoke about the young woman's divine destiny, her individual worth, and her struggles and temptations. She prayed that the young woman would be protected from the powers of the adversary until she could gain enough strength to withstand. It was a call for help, and as the prayer ended, I watched two sisters embrace and weep together.

That night a signal got through; the warning was heard. The young woman heard her adviser pray to our Heavenly Father in her behalf for her safety and her safe voyage through troubled waters. That night, as she heeded the warning and responded to the prayer of her adviser, many lives were saved—perhaps as many as lost their lives on the *Titanic*. For one young woman responding to the warnings can save generations. Her faithfulness provided increased safety for her children and her children's children for generations unnumbered.

"And now, if your joy will be great with one soul that you have brought unto me into the kingdom of my Father, how great will be your joy if you should bring many souls unto me!" (D&C 18:16.)

# Chocolate Chip
# Cookies

Waiting until you're sixteen to date seemed to Shelly like waiting
for the Millennium—she knew it would happen sometime but
probably not in her lifetime. The pain of waiting, she felt, was much
harder because she had such wonderful invitations she had to turn
down.

On one special occasion the invitation was left on her doorstep,
written in poetry. Shelly ran to her mother full of hope, but as she
read the expression on her mother's face, her faith wavered. "Oh,
mom, why didn't you have me born sooner?" she cried. Her mother,
with genuine concern for Shelly's plight, reminded her, "Shelly, my
dear, you were born six weeks premature. I did the best I could."
After a few tears and lengthy discussion full of whys, and with
encouragement from her mother, Shelly prepared a response to the
invitation. "Going with you to Homecoming would be like a dream
come true," she said. "However, you didn't say what year you
wanted me to go with you. I'm hoping it is for 1986. By then I'll be
sixteen, and going with you, I'll feel like the homecoming queen."

The response was painfully delivered and next year seemed so
far away. Would he remember her then?

In family home evening, the family members shared their challenges and concerns so that they could help carry each other's
burdens, as they had read in Mosiah in the Book of Mormon. The
scripture said that members of the church in Alma's time were
willing to mourn with those who mourned and comfort those who

stood in need of comfort. (Mosiah 18:9.) Shelly poured out her heart to mom and dad. It wasn't just waiting until she was sixteen to date, it was a lot of other things too. Why did her family have such strict rules? And how could she have friends if she couldn't go where they went and do the things they could do? What is wrong with watching an R-rated movie? Other kids do, and they're not bad. Is it wrong to hang around the mall if you don't do anything? Sometimes it seemed to Shelly that growing up was not much fun in the Larsen family.

Her parents listened, and they talked together as a family. There must be some way to ease the pain of strict parents and the challenges of the teenage years, and still be happy. Together they discussed a plan. Shelly's father suggested that they could finish a room in the basement where her friends could come. Her mother suggested decorating it with colorful posters, a record player, and a video recording, and serve ice cream, milk shakes, and sodas. It could be like a "Righteous Hangout," where friends would be welcome to come, but the standards for the music, the movies, and all activities would meet the family standards. Shelly wasn't sure her friends would be very excited about such a plan, but they decided to try.

The basement room was finished, and friends were invited over.

"I can't go with you, but you could come to my house," she would tell them. It was the offer of ice cream and milk shakes and sodas that seemed at first to attract the friends who dropped by. Soon it was a place just to come and talk about things that friends like to talk about with other friends.

Shelly's parents were always nearby to pick up the dishes, provide refills, listen to the kids' ideas and their concerns, and sometimes offer suggestions. It seemed to Shelly that some of her friends came not so much for the treats, but to have a mother and a father who would really listen, talk to them, and listen some more. One friend said, "It often seemed that the advice was more like a story given for you to figure out the meaning. It wasn't like preaching at all."

Shelly sometimes wondered if her friends came to see her, to eat ice cream, to play records, to talk together, or to be listened to by her parents and "get the word" from her mother. You see, her mother would quietly listen and then, sometimes later, would come up with a story that fit. One of the favorite homemade stories that she cooked up along with a batch of homemade chocolate chip cookies was called "The Tragedy at Rayad." It became a favorite story of the youth, who would gather around for storytime. Looking into the eyes of the group, Sister Larsen would begin:

Once upon a time there was a little kingdom called Rayad. The tiny people who inhabited this kingdom were called Rayadites. They lived happily, sharing and caring about each other. Life was good to them. There were only a few things they needed to watch out for; for instance, chocolate cake or wearing the color red. If any Rayadite ever ate chocolate cake or wore red, his spirit would become weakened and he would care less and less about himself and the rules of the kingdom.

Also living in this tiny kingdom was Zynock, an evil person who wanted to destroy the kingdom and all of the people in it. He hated for them to be happy and loving, for that made it harder for him to influence them. He knew what weakened their spirits and made them easier to capture. But Zynock also knew that he could not just offer the Rayadites chocolate cake and have them devour it—they were not that foolish! Nor could he make the most wonderful garment in bright red and expect them to wear it immediately. The Rayadites wanted to be good and strong. They had promised each other that they would help and strengthen each other in times of need. So how could Zynock weaken this people? How could he get them to succumb to him so that he could destroy them and thus the whole kingdom?

"Let's see," he said, "I can't get them to eat chocolate cake right off, but maybe I can get them to develop a taste for chocolate."

That's when chocolate chip cookies were introduced to the kingdom of Rayad. At first the cookies were ignored and scoffed at. Then some commercials and billboards were produced that showed handsome, wonderful-looking Rayadites eating chocolate chip cookies. And nothing happened to them, except they became more popular and sophisticated—at least that's what the message conveyed on the screens and billboards.

It wasn't long before a few Rayadites could be seen eating a chocolate chip cookie every now and then, and they seemed to be doing fine. They were still loving and caring and hadn't changed at all—so it seemed. So more and more Rayadites began eating the cookies. What they didn't realize was that the portion of chocolate chips in each cookie had been doubled. They were getting a double dose of chocolate, disguised in the cookie. You'd hear phrases like these: "That cookie is really good except for a couple of places where it tastes pretty chocolatey. But don't miss the cookie just for those two places. It's too good a cookie, and you can overlook the taste." "I heard that one of our friends has eaten a chocolate chip cookie and she says it's nothing to be afraid of. It won't ruin your life if you eat it!"

That was true: lives didn't seem to be ruined by chocolate chip cookies. Things were pretty much the same as usual. However, some of the teachers and leaders and parents in Rayad suggested avoiding the cookies because tastes for chocolate were being developed.

"Avoid the cookies?" came the cries of surprise. "What for?" "What's wrong with them? They're not chocolate cake!" "How stuffy can you get?"

Some who refused to eat the cookies were even laughed at and made fun of. Zynock himself started chuckling. He had no idea his plan would work so well. And Zynock was patient. He didn't care how long it took to destroy Rayad, just so it was destroyed.

Chocolate chip cookies seemed to be moving pretty well. Zynock didn't worry about the words of caution and counsel from the leaders, because his commercials and billboards were so exciting and enticing. He had to make them that way, or the truth of the leaders would have swayed the Rayadites away from the cookies.

Now it came time to introduce a new product of destruction. No, not chocolate cake, not quite yet. Rather, Zynock began advertising spice cake, white cake, yellow cake, carrot cake, any kind of cake but chocolate—but all with chocolate frosting, rich chocolate frosting. More commercials, more billboards, a few songs to hum and sing all day about how wonderful chocolate cake would be, although they're not eating it—yet! Get them thinking about it before they will actually succumb. Then in the kingdom of Rayad, you could hear:

"Have you tried that yellow cake with chocolate frosting?"

"Well, no. Is it good?"

"Oh, yes! Granted, it is chocolatey, but it's not chocolate cake. And it really doesn't have much more chocolate than those cookies we've been eating!"

"But the cake doesn't seem right. I mean, cookies are one thing, but cake?"

"Ah, come on! The important thing is the chocolate, and this is no more than you've already been eating. Everybody's eating it. You can't pass it up and be the only one left out."

In the meantime, the songs were subtly strumming away in the background, singing the praises of chocolate cake. Right, the words were not good, but the beat and the rhythm were so cool that many Rayads listened just for the music. After all, what can music do?

Zynock began thinking again: "One thing that strengthens those Rayadites is when they are together talking to each other. What can I do about that?" Then he reasoned, "Well, it's all right for them to be together. In fact, maybe there is some way I could use their gatherings and parties for my purposes. Aha! I've got it!"

So parties in Rayad began changing. Instead of the Rayadites talking to each other and playing games so they could get to know one another and share their strengths and talents, a new trend began. Everyone who was anyone had the new kinds of parties.

"Have you been to a party over at our Rayad friend's place yet?"

"No, I haven't."

"You should go. It's really cool!"

"Oh? What do you do?"

"Well, it isn't like any other party you've been to. It's pretty cool. All you do is go and sit down and watch stuff on the screen."

"Stuff on the screen? Like what?"

"Oh, exciting, scary stuff that's pretty good. There are a few scenes showing people eating chocolate cake, but no 'biggy.' "

"People eating chocolate cake? But..."

"Oh, it's not bad, and besides, there's nothing anymore without a little bit of that. It's just fun to get together with your friends."

So Zynock stood back and watched his plot unfold. "Let's see now. They're eating chocolate and they're eating cake. They're listening to songs and watching movies about chocolate cake. They're becoming weaker and weaker, although they're not even aware of it yet because they haven't actually eaten chocolate cake. They talk about it, make jokes about it, but they haven't eaten it—yet! They are falling into my trap! They think their leaders and parents are square and stuffy. It's very helpful when their friends tell them what I want them to hear. Friends are my greatest asset!"

"Hey!" says a friend Rayadite, "have you seen the latest movie?"

"No," comes the response. "I thought it was C-rated, for chocolate."

"No, it isn't. It's R-rated for Red. There's no chocolate in it."

And so Zynock continues his plotting—this time a gorgeous garment, but not in red . . . yet. It's a luscious pink color.

The tragedy at Rayad was just another "homemade" story, or so it seemed, and would soon be forgotten until one of the group picked up on the idea of calling their friend a Rayadite when any statements that sounded like a compromise were mentioned. Shelly began listening for Rayadite comments among her friends.

"That movie is okay. It is just the language, and you can overlook that," was one such comment. And in another setting she heard, "The music is okay. We just don't pay attention to the lyrics." From another friend she heard, "Oh, I know it's not good, but you can't say it's really bad." It almost seemed that the language of the Rayadites was becoming the popular language of the day among some of her friends. Just this week she heard, "It's not like lying. It's just like exaggerating the truth." And another comment: "Just this once. Everyone is doing it. Just once won't hurt."

The story had more meaning now; it was not chocolate chips, or the color red, or anything like that that really mattered. As she continued to hear Rayadite comments among her friends, the message her mother intended became more and more clear.

Maybe going to a dance before you are sixteen is not so wrong; maybe learning obedience without rationalizing at the age of sixteen makes all the difference. The story was not about chocolate chip cookies but rather about things that appear to be so desirable that you begin to rationalize and to justify. Shelly smiled to think of the wisdom of her parents. Their plan was working. The ice cream parlor was a setting for growing up while waiting to be old enough to be "Going Out."

# The Things That
# Matter Most

It was the last session of the youth conference just before the closing testimony meeting, the best part of all. I had not been able to attend the entire conference but had been there long enough to recognize that this group of young people seemed to have been abundantly blessed with material things. Their clothes were the latest fashion, and the labels on their shirts gave me reason to believe that these young men and women had developed a taste for the things that money can buy.

I wondered how my message would be received and whether or not I could get through to them with the valuable things that money can't buy. As the group gathered, I observed that there was a definite pattern to their seating arrangements. Some of the young men stood at the back near the doorway, as if to be ready for a quick escape in case of fire. Some of the young women entered and left, entered and left several times, as if to test the water before they were ready to make a commitment and jump in. When the young women finally took their seats, this was the signal for the young men at the back to make their final decision about where to sit. The few vacant benches and chairs left little opportunity for indecision.

The opening song was led by a woman who had obviously had some experience in conducting music. She captured everyone's attention and participation for "Shall the Youth of Zion Falter?" To that question the chorus began with a loud and strong response "No!" and continued: "True to the faith that our parents have cherished/True to the truth for which martyrs have perished." On the high notes, which left many without sound for their efforts, her voice rang out loud and clear until the notes descended and everyone could once again join in.

After the opening prayer and a generous introduction, I took my place at the pulpit. At that moment in a meeting, almost everyone is attentive and willing to withhold judgment as to whether they will give their full attention to the message until they get an idea of what it is going to be about. This is a critical time. If a speaker turns the audience off in that first minute or two, there may not be another chance, regardless of how interesting the message may be later on. I wanted to talk to these young people about values, about what matters most, and about how you decide. I knew that my introductory remarks had to catch them in a net of excitement, to try to hold them captive for the next forty-five minutes.

Without any warm-up or further introduction, I asked the audience how many of them had a brother or sister about three or four years old. This was somewhat of a surprise beginning; at least their curiosity got them involved for a time. Many of them raised their hands. I then asked how many of them thought they really liked their younger brother or sister. A few hands went down, but the big smiles probably indicated some childish pranks that had caused embarrassment. Looking over the first couple of rows, I called on one young woman who appeared to be confident and who had a big smile.

"Would you please come up?" I said, looking at her. "Me?" she said, pointing to herself. "Yes," I said. "Would you please?" There was a rustle among her friends, who wondered what she had volunteered for. Then she made her way from the center of the row to the aisle and up to the pulpit.

As she stood beside me, she obviously was also wondering. I assured her she would know all the answers to the questions I was going to ask in this brief interview. "Would you please tell us your name?" was my first question. "Shauna," she responded, smiling down at her friends. Her friends were returning broad smiles as they waited for the next question. "Do you have a younger brother or sister?" I asked. These questions were not too difficult, and she began to relax a bit. "A little brother," she said. "And what is his name?" "Richard," she said. "Is that what you call him?" I asked.

"No," she said, shaking her head. "We call him Ricky." "And do you really love your little brother?" I asked. A smile and a nod affirmed her love for her brother.

After that brief introduction, it was obvious that this was a great teaching moment. Every person in the audience was attentive, waiting to hear how one of their friends would answer these curious questions. And the questions became even more curious. By now Shauna seemed to be enjoying the attention she was getting from the audience. Poised and confident, she surveyed the entire gathering, smiling and capturing their interest.

I had remembered reading about an illustration that helps us determine our values, so I asked, "Shauna, do you know what an I-beam is used for in construction?" She hesitated a moment, so I explained. "I'm referring to a particular I-beam—one that is six inches wide and six inches high. It is made of steel and it happens to be 124 feet long. That is a considerable distance beyond the length of this building."

At this point we were talking together while the audience looked on. "Shauna," I said, "just suppose this I-beam six inches wide and six inches high was lying on the ground outside." She looked thoughtful, trying to envision this imaginary situation. I continued with further details. "Now suppose I am standing at one end of the I-beam and you are standing at the other, 124 feet away. I'm going to shout to you from where I am standing. 'Shauna,' I call, 'if you will walk all the way across the I-beam and don't step off, I'll give you one hundred dollars.' " Her smile broadened. "Would you do it?" I asked. "Sure," she said, without any hesitation, probably already having in mind just what she would do with an extra hundred dollars. The response from her friends assured her that she had definitely given the right answer.

"Now we're going to change the situation a little bit," I explained. "We're going to take this same I-beam all the way across the country to New York City. Have you ever been there?" She said she had. "Have you seen the tall twin towers of the World Trade Center?" Again she said she had, "Do you happen to know the distance between those two towers?" I asked. She shook her head. "Well," I explained, "those towers just happen to be 120 feet apart." Shauna's thoughts were racing ahead of the story, and she began shaking her head emphatically. I continued to explain this imaginary situation.

"It is a stormy day and the wind is blowing," I said. "The I-beam has been carefully placed at the very top of the twin towers, one end on one tower and one end on the other. Oh, yes, there is just one more detail you should know: The towers are 1,350 feet in the air." She was ready with her answer before the question was asked, but I proceeded. "Shauna," I said, "now just suppose you are on top of one tower near the end of the I-beam and I am on the other. I shout through the wind and the rain, 'Shauna, if you will come across this I-beam, I'll give you a thousand dollars.'" "No way," she said, "absolutely no way." I extended the offer with an additional amount: "How about ten thousand?" "Not for any amount," she said emphatically. "A million?" I offered. "Not ten million," she said. "I wouldn't do it for any amount." Her friends were listening intently.

"Then let me change the story just a little bit," I said. "This time we have the same situation: a stormy day, with the wind blowing, and you are at the top of one tower—but I am not at the top of the other." I paused, then went on. "By some tragic means, a person who has no respect for life and who has lost all sense of right and wrong has managed to kidnap your little brother, Ricky. This person is standing at the edge of the tower, holding your brother over the edge with his feet hanging in mid-air. He shouts to you, 'If you will come across the I-beam right now, you can save your brother.'" I hesitated a moment, then asked in a quiet voice, "Would you go?" With tears streaming down her face, she nodded. "I'd go." I looked at the audience and saw hundreds of young people who would have given the same answer. "I'd go." The tears in their eyes revealed something of their values, the things that matter most.

Shauna had spoken for all of them. It was not all the things that a thousand dollars or even a million dollars would buy that mattered most. Life is more important than taking a chance on the things that money can buy. And there is no price that can be put on a brother or a sister, or a friend.

"Thank you, Shauna," I said as she returned to her seat. To the audience I explained: "Shauna has taught you about values and what matters most in life, and how we can go about setting our goals in relation to the things we value most. When we know what our values are, we can easily decide what we will do and what we will not do—even what we would be willing to live and die for, if necessary. What would you be willing to do to insure that you and your family could be together forever?" I asked. "You know, our time is our life. And whatever we are doing with our time, we are paying for with our life."

I observed that some in the audience had caught that message, but some hadn't, so I turned to the scriptures and read: "Greater love hath no man than this, that a man lay down his life for his friends. Ye are my friends, if ye do whatsoever I command you." (John 15:13–14.) "Our Lord and Savior, Jesus Christ, gave his life so that we might live and have eternal life," I explained. "He asks us, 'Love one another, as I have loved you.' (John 15:12.) How can we do this?" I waited. There was a hush over the audience, as each person reached for his or her own answer. "Always remember," I explained. "Our time is our life. When we spend time with our friends, we are giving them part of our life. And when that friendship, that relationship, lifts, encourages, strengthens, and helps protect our friends from dangers that could threaten not only their physical life but even more important their eternal life, then we have something worth crossing the I-beam for, something worth giving our time for, because our time is our life. On the other hand, imagine choosing to spend our time, which is our life, on things of little value or no value. One earth life is all we have, and then it's gone."

These young people appeared to be listening not only with their ears but also with their hearts. We could all feel the Spirit that was present. For some, it may have been for the first time.

"And so it is," I went on. "When we know what we value most in life, we can write down our values. With our values in place, we can more easily make our choices each and every day. Our decisions will be determined by the things that we value most, the things we would be willing to cross the I-beam for."

In the audience that night I imagined I could see several hundred young people with their values in place. These were young people who would be as courageous as Shadrach, Meshach, and Abed-nego, whom King Nebuchadnezzar threatened to throw into the fiery furnace if they would not bow down and worship the golden image. These young men refused, saying, "If it be so, our God whom we serve is able to deliver us out of the burning fiery furnace, and he will deliver us out of thy hand, O king." Their commitments were so strong to the things they valued that they told the king, "But if not . . ." in other words, if we are not to be delivered, we will still not go against what we know to be right—our God and our values. And, as we know, the three men were cast into the fiery furnace. But when the king looked into the furnace, there were not three men but four. And they were not hurt in any way, and "the form of the fourth was like the Son of God." (Daniel 3:12–25.) Because of their values and their faith, they were spared.

In that same audience I saw many young women not unlike the three young virgins spoken of in the book of Abraham who were offered up on an altar. Because of their virtue, they would not bow down to worship gods of wood or of stone; therefore they were killed upon the altar. (Abraham 1:11.) Their integrity demanded that they make their actions consistent with their knowledge of right and wrong, and they could not do otherwise.

Our time together had come to a close. I had been in the presence of great and noble youth anxious to commit their lives to valuable things that money cannot buy. May this be the desire of all of our youth today!

# A Wallet Is
# Returned

"Will you please forgive me? I want to be honest," she whispered after handing me the familiar old wallet that had been taken nine years before.

With head bowed, she briefly explained that she had never stolen anything before or since. Then, as she turned to walk away, I heard a sigh of relief escape her lips.

Occasionally in a lifetime one experiences even with a stranger the reverent feeling of being in the presence of the truly pure in heart, and it was with this feeling that I fingered the worn wallet with the broken zipper. Memories of years gone by returned to mind with the clarity of only yesterday. Snapshots of special friends along with an activity card and other identification cards gave evidence that it was indeed my old wallet. I instinctively glanced into the pocket for the paper bills and was not surprised to find what appeared to be the very same ten-dollar bill that had been there the day I lost my wallet.

It had been nine years since, as a student at Brigham Young University, I had used the telephone in the Joseph Smith Building and had carelessly left my wallet in the phone booth. I returned to the lost and found department regularly for several days before finally giving up my desperate hope of ever getting my wallet and money back. That ten dollars was all the money I had, and I was in the habit of measuring my expenditures with great care. Without an understanding landlady, its loss could have caused some real problems. But that incident, like many others, faded into the background as more important memories crowded in.

Years had passed. One snowy afternoon the mailman delivered a rather fat envelope with two letters enclosed. The first one, from Mom, included a few questions about the other letter, which began: "To whom it may concern, anyone knowing the whereabouts of Ardeth Greene please forward this letter. It is very important that contact be made as soon as possible to settle some unfinished business at the B.Y.U." A name and an address were then given.

My first reaction was of indignation, since I knew of no unfinished business for which I was responsible. When my mind flashed back to my first experience with a bank account when I had written a check for groceries on the wrong bank, I became a little less indignant and wondered what unfinished business I needed to set in order.

With some anxiety I found in the Salt Lake City telephone directory the name of the person who had signed the letter. I quickly dialed the number and asked for the person by name. A pleasant voice responded, "This is she." I identified myself and began with some apologies for any unfinished business, only to be interrupted by an intense voice speaking rapidly as if to spill out all the words at once. She continued unloading her story until finally there was evidence of a burdened heart now relieved from foreign and contaminating elements too long contained.

It seemed that this young woman, now a wife and mother, had been in nurses' training at BYU. She had worked to put herself through school, but she needed an additional ten dollars for tuition, so she turned to her boyfriend for help. She promised to return the loan by Friday, but when Friday came, she was still short ten dollars, in spite of her earnest prayers.

Not knowing why, she had walked into the telephone booth and found an old worn wallet. She explained how her heart started to pound, since she'd never been tempted like this before. She held her breath when she opened it to find a single ten-dollar bill. Then the question: was this indeed an answer to her prayer?

She interrupted her steady flow of words to explain that since then she had learned that Satan knows when we are being tested and when we might weaken under pressure, and we can be sure he will be there if there is a chance we might fall.

Then, picking up the story again, she told of paying her boy-friend, whom she later married, finishing school, and now raising a beautiful family and rejoicing in the blessings of the gospel.

Her voice choked with emotion as she painfully related the details about the old wallet. She emphasized how she had been taught right from wrong and how she was well acquainted with the principle of honesty. Her conscience had prompted her, but she had listened to the wrong voice and had acted contrary to that which she knew was right. She explained how taking the money had seemed justified at the time, but for nine years her conscience had never been at peace. She told of her suffering for what she acknowledged as being a sin.

Elder Orson F. Whitney once wrote concerning sin: "Sin is the transgression of divine law, as made known through the conscience or by revelation. A man sins when he violates his conscience, going contrary to light and knowledge—not the light and knowledge that has come to his neighbor, but that which has come to himself. He sins when he does the opposite of what he knows to be right." (Quoted in Bruce R. McConkie, *Mormon Doctrine,* Bookcraft, 1966, p. 735.)

For nine years, through many moves, the old burden had lain deeply tucked away in this young woman's dresser drawer. Though she had considered throwing it away many times, it seemed impossible to do. There is no way one can throw away a wrong.

One day, while she was straightening the drawer, the old wallet surfaced again. This time she felt she must get rid of it, but in the right way. She had learned many valuable lessons over the years, and she had a quiet assurance that even this experience had served a purpose. She thoughtfully opened the wallet once again and examined it. This time her fingers uncovered a small orange card tucked away in a tiny compartment not previously noticed. This orange card would be the key to unloading her burden. On it was the address of a clinic in Calgary, Alberta, Canada, where a medical examination for a student's visa had been given.

With a prayer in her heart, she sent a letter to the clinic, addressed "To Whom It May Concern," and asking that it be for-warded, if possible. The letter was forwarded first to my parents in Canada and then back to Utah, where it finally reached its intended destination. Contact had been made, but the wallet was yet to be returned. During our telephone conversation she indicated the wallet would be mailed that very day.

When one sees in another a keen sense of right and wrong and a great virtue carefully tuned by the Spirit through struggle and final victory, there is a reaching out for association with that person, a desire to meet one so honest in heart. Thus I asked her if she would consider delivering the wallet in person. She seemed a little embarrassed at the request until I assured her it would be an honor and a privilege to meet a person who had such honesty of character. She agreed to meet me that afternoon at the office where I was working.

When I returned from lunch, the young woman was sitting beside my desk, with her back to me. Her shoulders were narrow but straight, and she sat erect on the edge of the chair with both feet squarely on the floor in front of her.

As I approached, she shifted nervously, then stood up. Then, as though she had rehearsed this experience in her mind a hundred times, she reached out a steady hand, looked me squarely in the eye, and handed me the wallet. Her steady gaze reflected the radiance of a good and honest life.

When she whispered, "Will you please forgive me? I want to be honest," my words would not come. I could only reach for her hand and nod affirmatively.

"Behold," the Lord has said, "he who has repented of his sins, the same is forgiven, and I, the Lord, remember them no more." (D&C 58:42.)

I went to the window and watched her turn the corner with a lilt in her step. Then, returning to my desk, I again heard the echo of her words. "Will you please forgive me? I want to be honest."

# Good Works

*Good
Works*

# A True Friend

Do you remember back when you were in the fourth grade? If you had been in my class right after lunch, we would have had a fifteen-minute story time, unless the story was so exciting that you pleaded to go on just a little further. Then it might have lasted twenty minutes, and on Friday afternoon, if it had been a good week, maybe even half an hour or so.

One of my favorite books to share with my students was *Charlotte's Web* by E. B. White. If you have read that book, you will remember that Charlotte is the spider and Wilbur is the pig. Poor Wilbur has some very hard times and often feels alone and discouraged. On one dreary rainy day, we read, he felt so "friendless, dejected, and hungry, he threw himself down in the manure and sobbed."

Have you ever had a Wilbur day? A day when you felt that alone and discouraged? Let me remind you of how Wilbur was rescued from his sad plight. He was visited by his dear friend Charlotte, the spider whom he didn't like at all when he first met her. But over the years he discovered a true friend in Charlotte, one who was willing to save his life by tirelessly spinning a beautiful web with a message that would let people know this was no ordinary pig. Even Wilbur began to believe he was something special because his friend told him he was.

At the end of the season, Charlotte knew that a spider's life is short and that she would not be around in the spring to comfort her friend Wilbur. She wanted to help prepare him for the future so he would learn to look for the good things and not be discouraged and lonesome. Charlotte spoke softly to her friend Wilbur: "Winter will pass, the days will lengthen, the ice will melt in the pasture pond. The song sparrow will return and sing, the frogs will awake, the warm wind will blow again. All these sights and sounds and smells will be yours to enjoy, Wilbur, this lovely world, these precious days..."

Charlotte stopped, and a tear came to Wilbur's eye. "Oh, Charlotte," he said. "To think that when I first met you I thought you were cruel and bloodthirsty!"

When he recovered from his emotion, he spoke again.

"Why did you do all this for me?" he asked. "I don't deserve it. I've never done anything for you."

"You have been my friend," replied Charlotte. "That in itself is a tremendous thing. I wove my webs for you because I liked you. After all, what's a life, anyway? We're born, we live a little while, we die. A spider's life can't help being something of a mess, with all this trapping and eating flies. By helping you, perhaps I was trying to lift up my life a trifle. Heaven knows anyone's life can stand a little of that."

"Well," said Wilbur. "I'm no good at making speeches. I haven't got your gift for words. But you have saved me, Charlotte, and I would gladly give my life for you—I really would." (E. B. White, *Charlotte's Web,* New York: Harper & Row, p. 164.)

Would you be willing to save a friend? Can you tell when a friend feels "friendless, dejected, and hungry," bad enough to throw herself down in a manure pile and sob? Some people do that, you know—not in the manure pile in the barnyard, like Wilbur the pig, but in the waste and filth of the world because they feel worthless, good for nothing. At times like this, we all need a friend, one who will tell us how special we are, one who will remind us of what President George Q. Cannon tells us:

"Now, this is the truth. We humble people, we who feel ourselves sometimes so worthless, so good-for-nothing, we are not so worthless as we think. There is not one of us but what God's love has not been expended upon. There is not one of us that He has not cared for and caressed. There is not one of us that He has not desired to save and that He has not devised means to save. There is not one of us that He has not given His angels charge concerning. We may be insignificant and contemptible in our own eyes and in the eyes of others, but the truth remains that we are the children of God and that He has actually given His angels—invisible beings of power and might—charge concerning us, and they watch over us and have us in their keeping." ( *Gospel Truth,* Deseret Book, 1974, p. 2. )

If you saw a friend in trouble what would you do? Read what one child did, as reported in a newspaper story:

"Brian Diaz, five years old, said he saw a neighborhood chum, three-year-old Andre Romero, enter the back yard of a vacant neighborhood home where there was a swimming pool.

" 'I followed him because I knew it was dangerous there,' Brian, a Phoenix, Ariz., kindergarten student, said. 'He was carrying a teddy bear, and then the first thing I knew, he fell in the deep end of the pool.'

"Brian said he lay down by the side of the pool, grabbed Andre by the hand, and pulled him out of the water onto the concrete decking. He said that Andre was heavy and that he almost fell in too. 'When he got out,' Brian said, 'it was like he was dead for a minute. He didn't say anything, and his lips turned blue. That water must be cold.'

"Brian put his hand on Andre's stomach and then pushed down as he had seen on T.V. 'Water came out of his mouth,' Brian continued, 'and then he threw up and started to cry.' "

A neighbor heard the cries and jumped the fence, then went to alert fire department paramedics. They treated Andre at the scene. The fire captain said that Brian "undoubtedly saved Andre's life." ( *Deseret News,* March 3, 1985. )

Would you be willing to save a friend's life? Sometimes that means calling for help, like the spiritual paramedics, those who have the love and concern but also the power and the authority to give blessings, comfort, and encouragement when people find themselves in trouble in the deep end of the pool, so to speak.

Following a talk at a youth conference, after everyone had shaken hands and few people were still around, I noticed one young woman standing some distance away. She had been waiting for a moment when she might speak in private. Together we moved away from the others into the seats near the rear of the chapel. The young woman, who was about fifteen, was serious and thoughtful. "I have a friend who is in bad trouble," she said. "She really needs help. What can I do?"

"Does your friend know that you know about her problem?" I asked.

"Oh, yes, she knows, but she would kill me if she ever thought that I told on her."

"How badly do you want to help her?" I asked.

"Well, somebody has to help her or she's going to make things even worse," she explained, "but what can I do? I'm not going to tell on a friend."

I was impressed with her sense of loyalty and her commitment to keep a confidence, but it was obvious that she also felt some responsibility for her friend, who was apparently in deep water over her head and perhaps even drowning. After some discussion, without her divulging any confidences, I asked several questions. It was evident that her friend was caught in the waste places of the world, in a manure pile like Wilbur, the friendless, dejected pig.

"If your friend were drowning, would you be willing to call a lifeguard? Or would you let her sink to the bottom of the pool rather than let anyone know she was in danger?"

"I'd call for help if she was drowning," the young woman said. "But I promised I wouldn't tell on her. She doesn't want people to know."

"Do you think she can keep her problem a secret forever? And if she could, is that what would be best for her?"

The young woman, thinking the situation through, said, "I think some people already know. Her parents must know something is wrong, but she won't talk to them. She just talks to me."

"In that case, you are carrying a tremendous responsibility on your young shoulders," I explained. "You need help because the weight will increase as you see your friend losing ground. I recommend that you seek help for yourself. Do you have a chance to talk to your bishop?" I asked.

"Sometimes," she said.

"Would you feel comfortable calling him and just telling him you have something you'd like to talk to him about?"

"Oh, I've never called the bishop. I don't know."

I realized that it would take a bit of courage for a young woman to call and make an appointment with her bishop, especially if she hadn't already had an opportunity to become friends with him. Her hesitation prompted another approach.

"How would you feel if I called and made an appointment with your bishop for you?"

"What would you say?" she asked. "I don't want the bishop to think I'm in trouble."

"I would assure him that you are not in trouble, but that you have a heavy responsibility and that you are striving to be a saint, a true disciple of our Heavenly Father. I would tell him that you want to be a true friend and to do only what is right, and you need his guidance. Now, you could talk to your parents or your friends or others, but the reason to call the bishop is because he is the one who can best help in times of serious problems, and you have a serious problem—a friend in desperate need of help."

Together we agreed that I would call the bishop and make the appointment for her.

"And what shall I tell him?" was her next question.

"Well," I suggested, "before you go for your appointment, talk to your Father in heaven about your friend. He already knows of her problem, and he still loves her very much. He wants her to be safe, and because she is your friend, he will guide you by giving you a feeling of peace in your heart about what you should tell the bishop and still keep the confidence and be a true friend.

"You might decide to tell the bishop that you have a friend you are concerned about and give him her name. That's like calling in the lifeguard to the rescue. When he asks you why you're concerned, you can tell him that you think she needs help and that you're trying to help her, but it's a big responsibility and you need help to know what you should do. If the bishop asks what kind of a problem your friend has, then you can be true to her and explain that the things she has shared with you are confidential. You can tell him, however, that you would be grateful if he would just call her in and talk to her as he does a lot of the other young people on their birthdays and at other times." I assured her that if she went with a prayer in her heart and a sincere concern for her friend, the words would come into her mind and she would know what to say and also what not to say.

Two weeks later I received a telephone call. It was the young woman who was concerned about her friend.

"Do you have a minute to talk?" she asked.

"I sure do," I said, anxious to get a report concerning the heavy responsibility she was carrying.

"Well," she began in a happy voice, "I talked to my bishop, and he really understood. He really wanted to help, and he didn't ask me to tell on my friend. He just asked if I thought my friend would come with me to visit with him sometime that week. He said he was talking to a lot of young people in the ward and wanted to talk to us. When I explained this to my friend, she was a bit hesitant and asked me if I had told the bishop about what she had done. I assured her that I had not. She decided that if I would go, she would go with me. It was almost as if she wanted help but wouldn't admit it."

She paused a moment, then continued. "We went to the bishop's office. It was kind of scary at first, but I knew we were doing the right thing. As soon as we walked in, the bishop shook hands with each of us. He was so warm and friendly, like nothing was the matter. Then he sat down beside us and began to tell us, without mentioning any names, the concern he has for some of the youth in our ward. When we looked into his eyes, we could feel his love for them and for us too. It was like he really cared. It was more like talking to a friend than talking to the bishop.

"The bishop told us about some of the problems that give him concern," she said, "and he asked for our suggestions and our help. Then he talked to us about how much he loves the youth, and how much our Father in heaven loves the youth, and how hard it is when Satan is working like never before to destroy each of us. I looked over at my friend and she began to cry. The bishop talked to us some more and taught us about repentance and forgiveness and how we can in time with enough effort overcome our weaknesses with the Lord's help, providing we are willing to do what he asks.

"When we were ready to leave, the bishop thanked us for coming in, and he told us that if we ever wanted to talk to him again or alone, he would be happy to spend some time with us. My friend was still crying. 'Would you like to talk to the bishop alone?' I asked her. She nodded her head. The bishop gave me a copy of the *New Era* and asked me to wait in the chapel while they talked. I sat there in the chapel waiting and praying that my friend would be able to tell the bishop all the things she had told me so that she could get the help she needed and so I wouldn't have to carry the load of knowing her problems all by myself. It seemed like she was there for quite a while, but I didn't mind waiting. I knew someone had come to the rescue of my friend. It was like Heavenly Father was there with us, and everything was going to work out if we worked together.

"That's what happened," she said, "when I called for help to save my friend."

I asked, "And how do you feel?"

"Wonderful," she said. "I feel that I have helped save my friend."

"Yes," I responded, in the words of Charlotte the spider, "you have been a friend and 'that in itself is a tremendous thing.' " Then I thought I could hear her friend respond to her in the words of Wilbur the pig: "You have saved me, Charlotte, and I would gladly give my life for you—I really would."

I like the words of a song by Michael McLean, titled "Be That Friend":

> *Your friends know what's right, and your friends know*
> *    what's wrong,*
> *And your friends all know sometimes it's hard to choose,*
> *But the friend who helps you see where the choices will lead*
> *Is the kind of friend you never want to lose.*
>
> *It's that friend who leads with love, doesn't push, doesn't*
> *    shove,*
> *Just reminds you of the truth you've always known,*
> *Then does more than just talk, takes your hand and starts*
> *    to walk*
> *By your side, along the road that leads back home;*
>
> *And this friend seems to see all the great things you'll be,*
> *Even when some things you do would prove him wrong,*
> *But he always believes that the real you he sees*
> *Is a champion he's simply cheering on.*
>
> *The love that you feel from a friend who's this real*
> *Is as powerful as anything on earth.*
> *For it lifts and it grows and it strengthens and flows,*
> *It's what allows a soul to feel just what it's worth.*
>
> *So many lonely souls are calling*
> *And our brightest stars would not be falling*

*If only they had a friend, a real friend.*
*Everyone hopes to find one true friend*
*Who's the kind they can count on forever and a day.*
*Be that friend; be that kind that you've prayed you might*
      *find.*
*And you'll always have a best friend, come what may.*

# He Ran All the Way

The chapel was filled to overflowing. People were still coming in, and additional seats were being added to the many rows that had already been set up in the cultural hall. From the back of the hall you could see over the crowd, but you had to stretch and bob your head back and forth around families who were getting settled in their seats.

The young missionary, supported on each side by her mother and father, must have felt deep gratitude for the numbers that swelled the normal attendance on this special sacrament meeting—one more faithful youth joining the ranks of those going out into the world to serve as special witnesses for Christ and search out the true in heart.

The last chord of the prelude music was sustained while the audience gradually quieted, and the bishop took his place at the pulpit. After a few words of greeting, he extended a special welcome to all the visitors, family, and friends of the missionary, and announced the opening song and invocation. The chorister had an unusual ability to lead the music with feeling and great dignity as the audience joined in singing "I'll Go Where You Want Me to Go, Dear Lord."

Following the prayer the bishop stood again and attended to some routine ward business. Then the tone of his voice changed from that of an effective and caring bishop to that of a loving father speaking to a beloved child. Looking out across the congregation as though there was only one of his flock he cared for at that moment, he spoke loud and clear. "Chad," he said. "Chad, are you here?" Immediately the sound of a folding chair knocking noisily against another could be heard, and other chairs were pushed back to clear the way, as people turned to identify Chad.

A young boy a few rows ahead of me made his way awkwardly into the aisle. His facial features showed some abnormality, and it appeared that he probably did not have the same mental abilities as other young people his age. He was facing life with some obvious handicaps, or so it seemed. I watched as this young man energetically, with great enthusiasm, literally ran from the back of the hall up the full length of the building, his short legs moving as fast as they could. He didn't slow down until he reached the steps leading to the podium. The bishop kept his eyes on the boy until he finally reached his side. Then putting his protective arm around Chad, he drew him close and the boy and the bishop looked at each other in a private exchange only they understood. Even strangers visiting the ward that day were impressed that this was surely not the first time the bishop had called and Chad had come running. They must have shared many private and important moments together before this hour.

With Chad nestled securely in the fold of the bishop's arm, they both faced the congregation. "Chad," the bishop proudly announced, "has earned his Duty to God Award. He has qualified in every way." Then, glancing down at the young man, he said with some emotion, "We are all proud of Chad."

The presentation was made, followed by the usual handshake and an additional warm and sustained embrace. But as Chad turned to leave, he broke with tradition and raised his hand high in the air, symbolic of what he had seen between good friends. A hand slap high in the air against the hand of a friend means friendship, team spirit, trust, good job, and a lot more. The bishop knew his boys and understood the signal. He responded to Chad's invitation by raising his hand to meet Chad's, giving a resounding slap in the air (and outside the meeting, he would have added the words "give 'em five").

Chad then turned from the bishop, but before leaving the stand, he moved awkwardly but enthusiastically toward the chorister, who stood and wrapped him in his arms. The audience witnessing this great happening wondered until we learned later that the man was his father. This special recognition was an award not only for Chad but also for his father and mother, waiting for his return in the back of the hall. The young hero left the podium, and made his way down the aisle wearing a broad smile, with his arm raised high in the air as if to "give 'em five" to every ward member who had been part of the team and was now sharing in the victory.

Looking around me, it was easy to identify those who were the visitors witnessing this ward family victory and those who were privileged to feel what Chad's accomplishments had meant to all who were blessed by the radiance of his personality.

It has been months since that memorable Sunday, but in my mind I keep playing that scene over and over again—not only with Chad as the star performer, the hero, but with every young man and every young woman who is playing a part so magnificently even when it is a struggle. Some have serious handicaps, not like Chad's but challenges of their own that they refuse to let discourage them, challenges that test their courage and strength, their commitment and ultimately their faith in a loving Heavenly Father.

The bishop calls. The call is heard. And in my mind I see every young person responding. Youths who have learned to listen for the call are prepared and ready, as was Chad. No one waits, no one walks, no one stops to explain, no one says why. However long the test or whatever the circumstances, however hard the handicaps, however steep the road, I see youths who are preparing to follow Chad's example and come running when called.

In this life we learn to listen for the call of the bishop, who is a representative of our Lord and Savior Jesus Christ. One day there will be another call, not from the bishop but from our Savior. A call to come home. The call will not come later, when we're better prepared, but now. We might hear the words, "Come, my child, come as you are but come now." We will each come with our limitations that became part of our test in this life, just as Chad came forward with his. We will not walk but, like Chad, will run forward, and each in our own time will return home. There our Father in heaven will draw us close in the protective fold of his arms. We will recognize him and he will know us, and we will receive our reward. And in that day, may we hear the voice of the Lord saying unto us, "Come unto me ye blessed, for behold, your works have been the works of righteousness upon the face of the earth." (Alma 5:16.)

# This Is All the Money I Have

The kindly old man didn't go outside as much anymore, and he didn't cross the street over to the Gardners' home as he used to. During the winter he had been there many times, not only to the Gardners' home, but also to the homes of neighbors up and down both sides of the street. After a heavy snowstorm he was usually out at the crack of dawn to clear the snow from driveways, providing a happy surprise in the early morning hours for grateful neighbors and friends. In the summertime he carefully arranged selected vegetables in baskets and carried them across the street to share with his neighbors. But it was not his vegetables that made him so popular with the children so much as the sweets he always had for them when they came around to the back door. His dear wife, restricted to a wheelchair, insisted on including "something sweet for the children" in their weekly shopping list.

Another winter season was slipping away, yielding to the warm sun of springtime. With this season came other signs of ebbing away. The old gentleman's garden had been planted with much difficulty this year. He tended it less often than usual, but enough, he hoped, to assure a good harvest that he might share one last time with his neighbors and friends. His good health was gone. His service to his friends was now greatly restricted. Some days were difficult and some were long for both him and his wife. "The very worst thing about being sick," he explained, "isn't the pain so much as the feeling of being so useless." He swallowed hard to keep the tears under control and forced a smile into the careworn lines on his face.

Across the street in the home of the Gardners, young Elizabeth, only seven and a half years old, had acquired a keen sense of concern for others. In her family, when anyone had a problem or felt unhappy, the family members discovered little ways to cheer each other up. Over her few short years, this child had seen her faithful mother find time to wipe a tear, heal a wound with a kiss, and listen to the never-ending account of a child who needed her attention. It was not just within the busy yet happy setting of her home that Elizabeth witnessed this activity. The same concern was expressed by her mother in many ways beyond her home, up and down the street, as the children distributed hot cinnamon rolls to many, or a dinner for a family on a special occasion.

One day young Elizabeth left her home quietly without telling anyone what was on her mind or in her hand. She looked both ways, then crossed the street. She was not carrying hot cinnamon rolls from her mother's kitchen as she had often done before. She came carrying her own treasures. She walked quietly through the carport overgrown with vines breaking into bud and made her way under the balcony to the back door with the little glass window in it. She rang the bell at the home of the kind old man and his dear wife, then quickly hurried to hide behind the large bush of Oregon grape.

Inside the home the old couple looked at each other and wondered who would be calling at this hour. The man, with some effort, eased himself up from his chair, stretched his back before taking a step, then shuffled toward the door. As he opened the door, his wife strained to hear a voice that she might identify. There were birds in the feeder that he attended to each day, but no one was in sight. He stepped out to look around, looking first one way, then the other, but there was no sign of anyone.

As he turned to come in, he noticed a torn piece of paper on the step by the door. It was a piece of newsprint, the kind he had seen children carry home from school. The paper had writing on it, and on top of the paper were two coins—a nickel and a quarter. Steadying one hand on his leg, he reached to the ground to pick up the note and the money. He could see that a message had been printed by a child.

By now his wife was calling, "Ted, is someone there?" She called again, "Ted?"

He shuffled back into the living room. "No one was there," he said in a quiet voice.

"Then what do you have in your hand?"

"Someone has been here," he said. "Look at this."

He sat beside his wife on the couch, and together, straining to see through their glasses, they read these few words: "Dear Mr. and Mrs. Greene, you are very dear friends of ours, you are always nice to us. Here is something you might need. From Elizabeth Gardner." Words barely hanging on the bottom of the edge of the page completed the message, "This is all the money I have."

Holding the paper in one hand, he opened his other hand to show his wife. There in the palm of a trembling hand lay the nickel and quarter. "All the money she has," he whispered, "a mite." His wife removed her glasses to wipe a tear from her eye and brushed a lock of gray hair from her forehead. "Like a widow's mite," he added. Together they sat holding the small piece of paper and two coins while they thought of a plan.

Walking with the help of a cane, Brother Greene made his way over to the Gardners' home, knocked on the door, and asked to speak to Elizabeth. She came to the door, her chin buried in her neck while she looked at the floor. The old man stooped over to wrap her in one of his arms while he steadied himself with his cane. Giving her a gentle hug, he thanked her for all she had done to make him and his wife so happy. The child smiled and looked up at her mother, who was now standing at her side, curious to know what her daughter had done. Elizabeth then told her mother about her visit to the Greenes.

"In our family we think of little things to do for people or give to them if they are feeling bad," she said. "We write notes to each other and leave little things like a cookie or a piece of candy. One time one of my sisters carved a little heart out of soap to go with a note she wrote to me when I was feeling unhappy." In a matter-of-fact tone Elizabeth added, "I got the idea from what we do in our family, and I decided to take it outside my family. I could see that Brother and Sister Greene were getting old, and I thought they might need to pay hospital bills or something." Then in a happy tone she concluded, "so I gave them all the money I had."

Now Brother Greene felt not so useless after all. There were still lessons to learn and people to serve. The following Sunday the aged man and the sensitive child visited with the ward clerk. "We'd like to make a contribution," they said, "a contribution of one nickel and one quarter to help build the new temple." The ward clerk was somewhat surprised. He was aware that each of them had made contributions individually, but the combined donation was a curious entry on the official form.

Brother Greene asked the ward clerk if they could have duplicate receipts so both he and Elizabeth would have one, but the clerk explained that only one receipt could be made. It was decided that she would get the receipt.

"I was so anxious for it," she later explained, "and it seemed like weeks before I got it. The day I received it, I took it over and showed it to Brother and Sister Greene. Brother Greene took me by the hand and led me over to the wall by his radio and showed me my letter, which he had framed."

A few months later Brother Greene passed away. As his treasures were being tucked away, the framed letter was removed from its place on the wall. Taped to it were a nickel and a quarter, reminders of the previous gift of a little girl who had given him all the money she had.

# White Carnations

The events of the past three days would be recorded in many journals as a youth conference never to be equaled. There had been several specially planned events and activities, lots of good food, and many new friends. The dance following the banquet was the last activity on Saturday. Sunday morning after the testimony meeting, which was always the highlight of the conference, there would be a brief evaluation meeting for the steering committee before everyone boarded the buses to return home. It would seem all too soon for many.

On Saturday night, Bradley, the conference chairman, came into the dance hall with two of his friends and motioned for me to come outside where we could talk without competing with the music. Outside was a small gathering of excited boys and girls, all talking at once. Their jumbled message might have been likened to the confounding of the languages at the Tower of Babel. Finally Bradley's voice could be heard above the others as he raised his hand, signaling his position as spokesman. "Let's start from the beginning," he said. With that signal, several interrupted, ready to begin again. "Hey, you guys, let me tell it, okay?" In a tone of excitement he asked, "Did you see Jennifer come into the dance?" Not waiting for my response, he continued, "She's in there now with a bunch of kids. She's okay," he explained with a smile. "She's all better."

Jennifer was a nonmember who had been invited to the youth conference by a friend. For the past three days she had often been seen alone or not at all. Her friend had deserted her, and it must have seemed that no one cared. She was terribly lonely. To be alone in a crowd of people is the worst kind of loneliness.

On Saturday, one of the conference workshops was conducted in a log cabin at the far end of a path leading from the lodge. In the subdued light of the cabin, a small group sat close together and talked about what our prophet had said concerning small acts of service and what that meant to each one individually. After openly sharing feelings that we all have—the need to be accepted and liked by others, and the need for approval and to be involved—the idea of small acts of service took on new and added meaning. It seemed quite possible that if everyone really tried to do some small act of service for someone, maybe miracles could happen right before our eyes.

According to the plan of the workshop, the youth, many of them almost strangers, visited in pairs while each one shared something praiseworthy he or she had noticed about the other one during the conference. The dialogue was slow at first, but soon the conversation picked up. During this brief time, while nearly everyone was deeply engrossed in sharing, I noticed two young girls sitting near a broken window, holding each other's hands. A tear could be seen on the cheek of the younger girl even though she was smiling, and I wondered what might have been shared, or if the two had known each other before. At the appointed time it was difficult to interrupt the many conversations to bring the group back together. It was evident that many small acts of service had taken place even in that few minutes.

Taking some chance, I asked the two young girls sitting by the window to come forward. A little bashful, but without hesitation, they came to the front of the group. After learning their names, I asked Melinda, the younger girl, what praiseworthy thing she had discovered about Pat.

She looked at Pat, smiling, as if waiting for her approval to share, then proceeded. "I'm almost the youngest one at this youth conference," she said. "My close friend who was coming with me couldn't come at the last minute, so it's really been hard." With that confession exposed, she dropped her head, her voice full of emotion. "On my way up the path to this workshop I felt so lonesome that I sat down on a big log and whispered a little prayer that someone, anyone, would be my friend." By now everyone in the group was feeling something of Melinda's loneliness. With tears rolling down her cheeks, she looked over at Pat and explained: "Pat came up the path through the trees. Many others had gone before her and some said 'Hi.' I thought she would do the same thing, but she didn't. She left the path and came over by me. I hadn't remembered seeing her before at the conference, but she asked me to come with her." There was silence for a moment, except for the whispering of the trees.

I waited, not wanting to interrupt Melinda's message, then asked, "Pat, did you know Melinda felt this way when you saw her?"

Pat shook her head. "No, not really, but I saw that she was alone, and she looked sad. I didn't know if I could help, but I knew she didn't have to be alone."

I inquired further. "How does it make you feel to perform a small act of service and be an answer to someone's prayer?"

Tears filled her eyes as she experienced the sensation of being in His service.

"Do you realize that you two are part of a little miracle?" I asked.

The two young girls, strangers until now, embraced in a bond of friendship.

We all felt the tenderness and the joy of someone being an answer to someone else's prayer. Each of us wished we had been the one who had stepped off the path instead of being among those who just said hi and walked on. The closing prayer was given by a young man, who prayed that we might all be more sensitive about small acts of service so that we might change lives, and perhaps even be an answer to another's prayer and create a miracle.

The youths and adults left the cabin, many of them wiping their eyes. Bradley was among the group; he left the cabin carrying with him a commitment to try to do little things that are really big things.

It was one of these big things that he was eagerly reporting under the lights of the parking lot just outside the dance hall. "It works," he said, over the strains of the music coming from inside. "It really works!" He continued his report. "You know, Jennifer didn't come to the banquet. The girls said she was sick, so she stayed alone in her bunk. I kept thinking of her in her room, probably alone, and it bothered me. I wondered what small act of service we could perform to help her. I wasn't expecting any miracle, I just wanted to help. Well," he said, "after we distributed one white carnation to each girl following the banquet, we had a few left over, so I thought, why not take what's left to Jennifer. I suggested it to some of the kids around me, and before I knew it, it seemed as if half of the girls had given back their carnations to add to the ones we all decided to take to Jennifer. The bouquet began to grow and grow until it seemed almost as big as the original bunch."

He continued enthusiastically, "We all headed toward the dorm trying to be quiet, but without much success. We decided that two of the girls would go in and bring Jennifer out for the presentation of the flowers. Karen and Phyllis went inside. We waited and waited. It must have taken a little persuasion, or maybe time to fix up, before all three girls finally appeared on the porch of the cabin."

One of the other boys spoke up. "It looked to me like Jenny might have been crying," he recalled, continuing the report. "Brad just stepped up to the porch, put his arm around her shoulders, placed this oversized bouquet of white carnations in her arms, and said, 'Jenny, we all want you to come to the dance.'" Then one of the girls in the group jumped in to report what she thought was the climax of the whole experience. Leaving out unnecessary details, she announced, "And she is in there right now dancing, and she says she isn't sick anymore."

Brad's countenance revealed much that was not spoken and that many would not have understood had he tried to explain. Standing in the shadows of the street light with friends who had been influenced by his suggestion, he radiated a light that reflected on the entire group.

The following morning in testimony meeting, deep feelings of gratitude and commitment were expressed by many, including Jennifer.

A brief evaluation meeting followed the testimony meeting. Bradley conducted, with adult leaders in a supportive role. From all reports the conference had been a great success. Bradley, as the youth chairman, had reason to express appreciation to the youth as well as adult committee members for the excellence with which they had accomplished their assignments. Then he invited me to comment. I asked him, "Considering all the experiences from the beginning of this conference to the very end, what would you consider the most significant happening?"

The young man, now having experienced the responsibility of a major leadership assignment, paused a moment, perhaps taking time to review in his mind the thrill of the day he was called into the stake president's office and asked to be chairman of the conference, or the excitement of inviting a nationally known entertainment personality to take part in it. In the moment he remained silent, we all waited, searching our own thoughts for what our answer might have been.

Now standing to his full six-foot-two height and looking straight ahead, almost as though he was not directing his comments to anyone in the group, he spoke from his heart. "If only you could have seen the look on Jennifer's face last night as she stood there on the porch when we took her the flowers. It was the happy look on her face—for me *that* was the most significant happening."

For Bradley it might have been the look on Jennifer's face that will remain with him. But for those who saw the look on Bradley's face at that moment, it was more than a small act of service he had performed—it was a miracle. "For inasmuch as ye do it unto the least of these, ye do it unto me." (D&C 42:38.)

*Good Works*

# Captains of Ten

"Are you the one who has been calling my daughter each week?" was the question.

The answer, from Keri Peterson of the Bountiful 29th Ward, Bountiful Utah Central Stake, was simple and direct, "Yes, I'm a captain of ten, and your daughter is on my team."

"Thank you," was the response from a grateful father. "Thank you very much."

The youth of this Bountiful ward were involved in a project called Moroni's Promise. It came in response to a challenge from Elder M. Russell Ballard given to the youth of the ward to adopt a meaningful and significant project for the year. This challenge was brought before the bishop's youth committee for discussion. The youth leaders decided that reading the Book of Mormon would surely be a meaningful and significant project.

One Sunday evening, all of the young people and their parents were invited to a meeting to launch Moroni's Promise. The young, valiant captains of ten gave the vision, reviewed the promise (see Moroni 10:3–5), spoke of agency and obedience, explained the program, and called for volunteers to join one of their teams.

One young captain of ten, Michelle Gardner, referred to a promise made by President Gordon B. Hinckley to all the members of the Church who read the Book of Mormon. He promised those who read daily that "there will come into your lives and into your homes an added measure of the Spirit of the Lord, a strengthened resolution to walk in obedience to his commandments, and a stronger testimony of the living reality of the Son of God." (*Ensign,* November 1979, p. 9.)

Appealing to the youth for whom she now felt a keen sense of responsibility, Michelle added her own personal testimony. "I know that when I read each day, especially when I study and don't just skim over what I'm reading, I do feel a greater desire to live the commandments and to have the Spirit of the Lord in my life."

Individualized packets that were provided included the quotation from Moroni printed on parchment ready for framing, a system for recording progress, recommended target dates, helpful study methods, a promise of "celebration stations," and a letter to be sent to a trusted friend or relative requesting support and continuous encouragement during the coming months as the participant read the Book of Mormon. An application form was also provided requesting the parent's signature as well as the signature of a member of the bishopric.

Each participant was invited to add his or her own signature as an indication of willingness to be diligent in endeavoring to reach the goal of having read the entire Book of Mormon within the set time limit. This could be accomplished by reading approximately sixteen pages each week. A captain of ten also signed the application indicating a willingness to be in touch each week to determine progress and provide encouragement to each member of his or her team.

Individual progress was not a public matter. However, increased interest was awakened when the aggregate scores of the teams were recorded on an attractive chart that was periodically displayed in the chapel foyer with pictures of various activities.

As eager participants finished the last verse of Alma 63, "And thus ended the account of Alma," they would rush, regardless of the hour, to Sister Bonnie Guthrie, who helped with the records, assisted in making calls for captains as needed, and dispensed T-shirts to each one finishing the book of Alma. The T-shirts with "STOMP" (for "Students Trying Out Moroni's Promise") printed in bold letters across the front provided the incentive that urged many through the pages of Alma.

A "celebration station" was an event scheduled at regular intervals along the way to give strong incentives and provide continuous encouragement to the captains, who in turn inspired their team members as they made their weekly contacts. The captains would then give an accounting to the specialist in a brief weekly meeting following sacrament meeting. Many, many extra calls at various times were required to accomplish this necessary follow-up.

As the group completed Alma, a celebration station was scheduled. The snow had been falling all night, and it was unseasonably cold, but nothing would daunt the plans for the scheduled tree planting celebration. A flowering cherry tree had been selected. The hole was dug, and ward members were invited to gather at the church.

Robert Davis stood before the group holding a scroll containing all the names of those who at that time had finished reading Alma. He rolled the scroll, put it in a plastic-coated container, sealed it, and then placed it in the hole at the base of the tree and explained, "You're probably wondering why we are planting a tree. If you will recall, in Alma the planting of a seed that became a tree has meaning because of the analogy to a growing testimony." He then read Alma 32:27–41: "But if ye will nourish the word, yea, nourish the tree as it beginneth to grow, by your faith with great diligence, and with patience, looking forward to the fruit thereof, it shall take root; and behold it shall be a tree springing up unto everlasting life."

On Mother's Day following sacrament meeting, the entire ward was invited to gather around the flagpole for yet another celebration station. Richard Newman and Mike Bettilyon, both captains of ten, unfolded a beautifully designed flag with the large dark blue letters "Moroni's Promise" centered in a white open field.

There were other names on the flag also. Those who had finished the book of Helaman had added their signatures to the flag as an official Mother's Day record. Bishop Bradford reminded everyone of the stripling warriors who did not fear death, for they had been taught by their mothers that if they did not doubt, God would deliver them. (See Alma 56:47.) The captains attached the flag and pulled the ropes, raising it to the very top of the long metal pole. Hearts were opened and feelings were tender, as expressed by a younger member of the group, who whispered to a friend close by, "My name is on that flag," and his friend responded reverently, "So is mine."

By now the flowering cherry tree planted earlier was bursting into bloom nearby as a reminder of growing testimonies.

What difference has all this effort made? There were 120 readers—38 adults and 82 youths—participating in Moroni's Promise.

Thirteen-year-old Wid Covey, standing before an audience, volunteered his testimony: "I'm thankful for this Moroni's Promise program because it helps me understand the scriptures. When I sit down with my dad to read the Book of Mormon, he helps me understand about it also. I'm thankful for Michelle Gardner. She calls me every week and encourages me."

Sister Margaret Kirkham reported, "Our whole family looks forward to Richard Newman, our captain of ten, coming to encourage us. This project has been a great influence to our entire family."

Bishop Bradford reflected on the program: "It has made a great difference. There are few activities that could have unified our youth as well as this. I can't say that all our young people now have strong personal testimonies of the Book of Mormon, but it's a super beginning. With the help of this inspired program, a great number of young people will be better missionaries in every aspect of their lives, and all of them are better prepared to withstand the evils of the world."

# Integrity

# Reaching Beyond

Shortly after a Young Women's satellite program where the speakers emphasized the importance of standing up for what you believe in, I learned about a young woman named Melanie. She was with a group of friends who had attended the satellite program, and one of her friends had brought an R-rated videotape. As they were about to put the tape on, twelve-year-old Melanie stood before the group and said, "Hey, you kids, we made a commitment to stand for truth and righteousness, and I'm not going to watch this. If I have to stand alone, I will." As a result of Melanie's integrity, none of the girls watched the videotape.

When I'm asked what is the role for LDS women, I think of Melanie. She has made a choice in her life to stand up for truth and righteousness, as have many other Latter-day Saint women of many ages. At twelve, she has made a commitment to righteousness and truth in her life.

I think we sometimes look at women in a very narrowly defined role. What is the "role" of a Latter-day Saint woman? It is not complicated at all. It is simply to be a righteous woman.

A righteous woman is well grounded in the principles of the gospel. She sets her priorities according to these principles and seeks to make decisions through inspiration. She understands that the Lord has a purpose for her life, and she desires to find and magnify that purpose. She is spiritually self-reliant.

Every woman can become a righteous woman, if she is willing to live what she believes. Her foundation of the gospel and the knowledge that she is a daughter of her Heavenly Father will help her to make righteous decisions, to choose that path for herself, whether she is single, married, divorced, a single parent, working at home or in the office, facing complex or simple decisions. Her bedrock is the gospel of Jesus Christ.

If there is a cause that is worthy of the righteous woman's life, she will stand up in any situation in defense of that cause. And when the cause is based on eternal values that are linked to the gospel of Jesus Christ, she will *live* for it, not just be willing to die for it. It is ingrained in her life with such conviction that no matter what the pressure, she can say, I will choose what I know to be right.

The world sends us different messages, though, about the so-called role and importance of women. Through advertisements, styles, television, movies, posters, it tells us that to be attractive is of utmost importance. The world measures beauty in terms of attractiveness to men. Thus, a woman is told that the more dates, the more boyfriends she has, the greater her worth.

This is a false standard. And it leads to many problems—anorexia, bulimia, lower moral standards, preoccupation with clothes and money, and low self-esteem. I recently read in a study that half of today's young women have low self-esteem. I believe this is a result of their trying to meet a standard that is both unrealistic and not founded in that truth which brings real worth and happiness.

We know through the prophets and scriptures that each woman comes from divine parentage and has inherited divine qualities that she can develop. Her worth is not dependent on the changing styles or whims of society. She is of infinite worth, with her own divine mission from the Lord. As she strives to find out what that divine mission is, and makes the effort to study the gospel and do the work of the Savior here on earth, she can become more like the Savior.

Eventually, in the eternal plan, every righteous woman should have as her ultimate goal to be a wife and mother. But the realities of our day are such that some of our young women won't have that opportunity at the time they may anticipate or want it. It then becomes very important that each one have intermediate—not other, not conflicting—goals that are consistent with her unique mission in life. And, of course, all learning and experience in any righteous endeavor prepares her ultimately to be a better wife and mother. Nothing should stand in the way of that goal, but what a tragedy it would be if our young women just waited around for that experience and then came to it empty.

One area in which a righteous woman needs to prepare is education—both spiritual and secular. Sister Camilla Kimball has said, "What we must be concerned with is preparation for life, and that preparation is continuing education. Whether it is to earn a living or to rear a family, men and women both need to have the knowledge that enhances their natural talents." Preparation for life is for both—women who marry and those who may never marry. It is for women who will have children to help educate and others who will not. It is for women who will need to support themselves and their children at some time in their lives.

President Gordon B. Hinckley said in a recent Young Women's fireside talk, "Never before in the history of the world has there been a time when so many opportunities have been open to women. Now is the season to train your minds and your hands for the work you wish to do. I am not suggesting that all of you should be university students. There is a need for technicians of many varieties, and the work to be done is honorable and contributes immensely to the society of which we are a part.

"Some of you may think that marriage will take care of all your future needs. Marriage is important, and I hope that each of you will have the blessing of a happy marriage, but circumstances arise in the lives of many women that make it necessary to work and provide for their needs. Education can prove to be the wisest and most profitable investment you can make. Get all the help and direction you can concerning your aptitudes and ambitions, and then get training to sharpen your skills and improve your opportunities."

As women develop the divine gifts within them, to realize their potential in growing in learning and wisdom, strengthening families, the Savior will be there to guide them, love them, watch over them, help them to progress and learn. As the Savior promised, "Draw near unto me, and I will draw near unto you." (D&C 88:63.) Righteous women will have many opportunities for their wisdom, voice, and vote to make a difference.

# A Friday Night Date

Your immediate concern may be a decision about a date for a party this Friday, and yet your decisions concerning dating have something to do with generations long before your time and also future generations for years to come. It is a big decision! Come back with me in time and we will work our way forward to the date, the boy, the place, the time, and your decision about your date this very week. Be patient. It is a rather long story because it goes so far back, but you will discover what all this has to do with your date this very week.

As members of The Church of Jesus Christ of Latter-day Saints, we are a covenant people. Understanding what that means is at the very heart of all our decisions, including your date this week and next. Let me explain. Our Father in heaven sent one of his strongest spirits to earth. His name was Abraham, and you and I are descendants of him. He is our great-great-grandfather many generations back. We are numbered with his posterity. Abraham was tried and tested. He was even commanded to offer up his only son, Isaac. The Lord knew that he could depend on Abraham. Only after he had proven Abraham's obedience was Isaac spared.

Through Abraham, the Lord was able to establish a covenant people. He promised, or covenanted, with Abraham that all his descendants would belong to the House of Israel, and all those who accept the gospel and keep his commandments would inherit the blessings of eternal life, the greatest of all the gifts of God. For this reason Abraham was very anxious that his son not take a wife from among the Canaanite women in the area who were out of his faith. So he commissioned his servant to go on a long and uncomfortable journey to obtain a companion of Isaac's faith. The servant took ten camels and departed.

When the servant arrived at his destination in a far country, he needed to know who was to be the companion for Isaac. He asked for the Lord's help, saying, "Let it come to pass, that the damsel to whom I shall say, Let down thy pitcher, I pray thee, that I may drink, and she shall say, Drink, and I will give thy camels drink also; let the same be she that thou hast appointed for thy servant Isaac; and thereby shall I know that thou hast shewed kindness unto my master." (Genesis 24:14.)

And before he had finished speaking, Rebekah came to the well. She was beautiful. The servant ran to meet her and said, "Let me, I pray thee, drink a little water of thy pitcher." And she said, "Drink, my Lord." She gave him some water from her pitcher, then she drew water for all his camels. (Genesis 24:15-20.)

The servant then inquired of Rebekah's father if she would go with him. They called Rebekah and asked, "Wilt thou go with this man?" And she said, "I will go." When they returned to Isaac, he was out in the field and saw them coming. The servant told him all that had happened. "And Isaac brought her into his mother Sarah's tent, and she became his wife; and he loved her: and Isaac was comforted after his mother's death." (Genesis 24:61-67.)

Rebekah and Isaac were true and faithful to the covenants they made with the Lord, and they yearned for their children to be true also, so that they might enjoy the blessings promised to those who are true to the faith. They had two sons, Jacob and Esau. Esau, however, married outside the faith. One day Rebekah, in great anguish and concern for their posterity and the need to have their children marry in the faith, said to Isaac, "I am weary of my life because of the daughters of Heth [Esau's wives]: if Jacob take a wife of the daughters of Heth, ... what good shall my life do me?" (Genesis 27:46.)

Jacob married in the faith, and his name was changed to Israel. He had twelve sons, and all his faithful descendants became members of the House of Israel, the covenant people. Those of non-Israelite lineage, commonly known as gentiles, are adopted into the House of Israel when they join the Church and become heirs of the covenant of Abraham, through the ordinances of the gospel.

As members of The Church of Jesus Christ of Latter-day Saints, we are descendants of Abraham, a chosen people, a covenant people with promised blessings, including the ordinances of celestial marriage. Each one of us has a divine mission and an eternal destiny. But to qualify, we, like Abraham, must be tried and tested. We must be given our choice, our agency, and be proven in all things.

When you fully understand the meaning of being of the House of Israel, a covenant people, you can better understand how your choices about dating become a matter of eternal consequence: Your decision regarding eternal marriage is the link that unites generations past and future, so your decision matters very much.

So we are here, in earth life, with many tests along the way. And what of a young woman who is sixteen and who has an invitation from a young man who is popular and gentlemanly but is a gentile, a nonmember? A prophet has spoken, saying, "Marrying outside the faith has always been forbidden." (Spencer W. Kimball, *The Miracle of Forgiveness,* Bookcraft, 1969, p. 240.) President Ezra Taft Benson reiterated this counsel in speaking to young people in 1986: "Clearly right marriage begins with right dating. A person generally marries someone from among those with whom he associates, with whom he goes to school, with whom he goes to church, with whom he socializes. Therefore, this warning comes with great emphasis, Do not take the chance of dating nonmembers, or members who are unordained or faithless. A girl may say, 'Oh, I do not intend to marry the person, it is just a fun date.' But one cannot afford to take a chance on falling in love with someone who may never accept the gospel."

Just as Abraham and Rebekah were concerned about their sons marrying in the faith, so it is that you also carry the responsibility of celestial marriage if your relationship is to be eternal and your children are to be born under the covenant and sealed in the temple as an eternal family.

Young men and young women who live in areas with few or no members of the Church can be a strong influence for good and help spread the gospel by example as they associate in social groups with their nonmember friends. Invite them to activities at church and to family home evening. Participate in school activities with young people who have high moral standards. Through friendship and association they may be led to a knowledge of the gospel and even baptism. This should come through group participation and not single dating.

You are probably shaking your head by now and wondering if all this must be rehearsed and reviewed before you respond to the date for this Friday. Let me assure you that is not the case. Once you have made the decision to marry in the temple and receive the blessings promised there, and to bring those blessings to your children who will be born under the covenant, then you have the answer to enticing invitations, even this week and next.

This decision takes moral courage, but it may also provide an example from which other young women may draw strength and be led to conduct their lives in harmony with the covenants they too have made. And while you may feel you stand alone because of your knowledge of your divine destiny as a member of the House of Israel, chosen of the Lord and reserved for this time, there are thousands of young women who are demonstrating the same moral courage and saying no when it would be so much easier to say yes.

President George Q. Cannon tells us what we might expect by way of tests. He says, "If there is a point in our character that is weak and tender, you may depend upon it that the Lord will reach after that, and we will be tried at that spot for the Lord will test us to the utmost before we can get through and receive that glory and exaltation which He has in store for us as a people. When we think about the character of the exaltation promised unto us, we can understand why this should be the case." (*Gospel Truth,* Deseret Book, 1974, 1:103.)

I believe that when a young woman at age fifteen and a half has an invitation to a special dance from a most desirable young man, and all of her friends, both members and nonmembers, are accepting dates to that special event, the Lord is mindful of her test at that very moment in life. To go or not to go is the question. If you go, then what? If you don't go, what? If you choose not to go, you'll miss the dance, and you will suffer, maybe even pain, a hurting inside at a time when friends, popularity, and acceptance are so crucial to your sense of well being. But it is a moment provided for enormous discovery about yourself, your love for the Lord, and the use of your agency at a time when it really matters.

There is no way to explain, before you make the decision, how you will feel after. Self-confidence, self-esteem, and increased faith are the rewards for obedience to the commandments. It may be easy to argue and say, "Well, if I'm almost sixteen, what difference does it make?" The matter at this point may not have as much to do with dating as it does with obedience. And obedience at one time can become a source of strength for more challenging times later on. Self-discipline in matters along the way prepares us for the very tests and purposes for this mortal life. President Kimball stated: "Any dating or pairing off in social activities should be postponed until at least the age of sixteen or older. And even then there should be much judgment used in selection, and in the seriousness. Young people should still limit their close contacts for several years since the boy will be going on his mission when he is nineteen years old." When social pressure is strong and desire is so intense, one cries out and asks, "But is it a commandment?" And then we listen again to the words of our late prophet-leader, President Kimball: "So we say to all youth, regardless of what country is your home, and regardless of the customs of your country, your Heavenly Father expects you to marry for eternity, and rear good, strong families. The Lord planned that men and women would find each other and have a happy family relationship. Be true to each other and remain clean and worthy. Now is the time for you to plan good, strong marriages, and organize your programs, and set your standards, and solidify your determination to prepare for that married period of your lives which will be beautiful and rewarding."

A custom in some areas is that of going steady. This implies a level of commitment to each other, an expectation of loyalty to one person at the exclusion of others. This arrangement is detrimental at an early age because it limits friendships, and of even greater concern is the increased seriousness of the relationship, which goes contrary to the prophet's admonition to "limit close contacts for several years." It increases the risk of developing intimacy, which threatens the loyalty to eternal covenants, to keeping the commandments, and imposes temptations, which Satan uses to get people into his net, for he desires that all men might be miserable like unto himself. Of steady dating, President Kimball said, "Dating in the early teenage years leads to early steady dating with its multiplicity of dangers and problems and frequently to early and disappointing marriage." Youthful dating is not uncommon and is often done with parental approval. Yet it is near criminal to subject a tender child to the temptations of maturity. Early marriages, which are almost certain of failure, are usually the result of steady, early dating, whereas a proper preparation for marriage is a well-timed courtship.

And so now, about the date for this week, what will your answer be? You must decide. And even after the decision has been made, the test will continue for a time, and it is usually by your closest friends, whose approval you yearn for. It comes in a form like this: "How come you are not going? Everyone else is. It's not that bad. We're not going to do anything wrong. Do you think you're better than we are? What's the big deal? Our parents are letting *us* go. We'll help you talk to your mom."

To the question from friends, why do you do what you do?, the answer may simply be, Because I know what I know. And while you may have to wait for the proper age or for an invitation from a member of the Church before accepting a date, you can have many friends, young and older, members and nonmembers. And into your mind will come the sweet refrain from the last lines of the song "I Walk by Faith": "And someday when God has proven me, I'll see Him face to face, but just for here and now I walk by faith."

# Who Will Take
# a Stand?

There were a lot of children in our neighborhood. On Sundays when they all congregated at the church, it appeared that the ratio of adults to children was ten to one in favor of the children. But in spite of the number of friends that might have been available on regular weekdays to play in the sun and never come in the house except for peanut butter sandwiches or a bathroom break, four-year-old Betsy would frequently abandon her playmates, make her way down the street, and knock on our front door.

I could always recognize Betsy's knock. It was more like the pounding of her hand three times, a brief break, and then once again and again until I could get to the door. "I'm coming, I'm coming, Betsy," I would say to myself until I could get to the door. There she would be in her well-worn sneakers, knees skinned from trying to keep up with the older kids, a scab on her sunburned nose. Her blond hair was bleached even whiter than usual, and her fair skin had gradually turned from mayonnaise white to gingerbread brown. She had purpose in her visit and immediately announced her request. "Can your daddy come out and play?" I had tried on previous occasions to explain to Betsy that my "daddy" was not my daddy at all but was my husband. That attempt was never successful, and the word *husband* in place of *daddy* was of little concern to Betsy. It wasn't the right word that held any interest for this four-year-old; she simply wanted to know if my "daddy" could come out and play.

174

By now my "daddy" was at the door to speak for himself. Tousling her curly blond hair, he agreed that his "mommy" would let him come out for a while if they could work in the garden pulling weeds together. There was no delay. She grabbed hold of his big hand, and pulled him after her to the garden where they had been weeding the day before. Occasionally I would go out to catch a bit of their conversation, which seemed endless.

One day I had returned to my work in the kitchen, and in less than ten minutes I heard Betsy's pounding on my front door again. This time, instead of repeating the pounding until I could get to the door, she came bursting in, her eyes wide and her mouth talking so fast I could not understand what she was trying to tell me. I knew it was something about my "daddy." "What is it? What is it?" I asked, grabbing her hand and running to the garden. Finding her playmate all right, I said slowly, hoping to calm her down, "Betsy, tell me one more time, and speak slowly so I can understand." She repeated her message slowly and with great feeling, pointing at her gardening partner: "He said a naughty word." Heber, sitting on the ground with his arms wrapped around his legs, was trying to contain his laughter.

Since I had been summoned to address Betsy's accusation, I began my questioning. "What word did he say?" I knew, of course, that the word in question was only naughty in her mind. However, that in itself made it a matter of great consequence.

Betsy was prepared to give a full report. She stood close to the accused, pointed her finger directly at him and announced, "He said I was full of malarkey."

"Malarkey?" I repeated, trying to conceal my laughter as I watched the accused waiting for the verdict. "And what does that word mean?" I asked.

"I don't know," she said. Being in full control of the situation, she pointed to him and said, "You ask him."

I continued the investigation, this time addressing the offender. "And what does that word mean?" I probed.

"Well," he pondered, trying to reach back in his mind to its origin. "It's a word my grandpa used to use a lot. It means full of fun, a little mischief, and lots of love."

I had been standing between the accused and the accuser, but with the additional facts related to the case, Betsy threw her arms around her friend, forgave him, and I was dismissed.

And now, years later, when I occasionally find myself in a shopping mall or a theater, in the halls of a school, or even in private where a group of young people are talking together, I hear words that come from their lips and I feel much as Betsy did when she came bursting into my house to put a stop to "naughty words." I want to take a stand in the middle of the mall, the theater, the corridor, or wherever, and call a court into session with the same fervor Betsy exhibited in her concern for words that sound offensive and wrong, inappropriate and immoral.

"Who will take a stand and speak out loud and clear in defense of purity of the mind and clean speech?" the judge would ask. Every youth would be called to the witness stand, courageous youth that I have met throughout many parts of the world. Someone in the group would speak up, even risk persecution from peers, and offer a challenge. "Try this, if you will," he would say. "Can you think of anything without formulating the thought in your mind by the use of words? Words form our thoughts. Good words—good thoughts." There would be those who would walk away from the gathering in disgust, but I believe that most would stay.

Another youth, a young woman this time, would take the stand and raise her voice in defense of truth and righteousness. "It is unrighteous," she would say, "to speak words that are vulgar, crude, and blasphemous. It is unfair to yourself and to your friends to allow the word pictures created by vulgar language to become part of your mind and pollute the air."

With this evangelistic call for support of clean language, another young woman in the crowd would move closer and wait for her turn to lend support to this great cause. "Our thoughts are the substance that fill our minds and make us who we are," she would testify. "The scriptures remind us that as a man thinketh, so is he. We become what we think about. We are what we have programmed our minds to be. A righteous person is righteous because he or she has chosen righteous thoughts that lead to righteous actions."

Another person would quote this wise thought: "Every thought we think, every conscious or unconscious thought we say to ourselves, is translated into electrical impulses which, in turn, direct the control centers in our brains to electrically and chemically affect and control every emotion, every feeling, every action we take, every moment of every day." ( *What to Say When You Talk to Yourself,* Scottsdale, Arizona: Grindle Press, 1986.)

The next youth to take the stand would be a little older and thoughtful in her counsel. "Can't you see," she would plead with her friends, "vulgar language is not sinful because someone thinks it should be avoided, but rather it should be avoided because it is sinful."

The next defendant for pure thoughts and clean language is a black woman, Jamie Noit. She is not part of my imaginary campaign against swearing, vulgarity, and foul language. She is a real person, speaking to all who will hear. Her words come from the *Ebony Rose Newsletter:* "The world knows how we are supposed to live. Instead of swearing outright, do you spell the word? (The Lord knows how to spell too!) We cannot hide from the responsibility we have to be openly on the Lord's side. If you're fortunate, you won't hear the cock crow three times to know when you're off the track. . . . Be not afraid to stand up for what is right. People who influence thousands need all the help they can get. If you don't say anything about something you don't like, it will continue to fester inside you. Silence is a form of agreement."

There will always be those who will persist, saying, "Show me where it says my language is so wrong." And there is further evidence to bring forth. In the heading to the third chapter of James in the LDS edition of the Bible we read, "By governing the tongue we gain perfection." And in verse 10 we read, "Out of the same mouth proceedeth blessing and cursing. My brethren, these things ought not so to be." (James 3:10.)

The question remains for each generation: Who will take a stand and pound against the door in a fight against "naughty words" with the same intensity as little Betsy?

Elder Dallin Oaks, an apostle of the Lord Jesus Christ, has spoken to youth and adults alike on this matter. He says: "A speaker who employs profanity or vulgarity to catch someone's attention with shock effect engages in a babyish device that is inexcusable as juvenile or adult behavior. Such language is morally bankrupt. It is also progressively self-defeating, since shock diminishes with familiarity and the user can only maintain its effects by escalating its excess. Members of the Church, young or old, should never allow

profane or vulgar words to pass their lips. The language we use
projects the images of our hearts, and our hearts should be pure. As
the Savior taught, 'Out of the abundance of the heart the mouth
speaketh. A good man out of the good treasure of the heart bringeth
forth good things: and an evil man out of the evil treasure bringeth
forth evil things.' (Matthew 12:34–35.)" (*Ensign,* May 1986, pp. 49–50.)

I see young women prepared to take a stand in defense of purity
in thought and word and who will pound against the door if
necessary to eliminate profane or vulgar words from the language of
youth in these latter days. I hear young women sing the song of the
rising generation:

> *Ask me, "Who will take a stand?*
> *Who will live the Lord's commands*
> *And bear the standards of a world to be?"*
> *With a promise firm and clear,*
> *I proclaim for all to hear:*
> *"I will, I will, send me."*
> (Janice Kapp Perry, "The Rising Generation")

*Integrity*

# She's My Sister

Two sisters sat close to each other on the leather-covered sofa in the outer office, whispering words of encouragement to each other. "You can go first if you want to," Linda told her younger sister. Mary was thoughtful for a moment. "I really think you should go first. It will be better that way." Then, with intensity in her voice, she touched her sister's arm and added, "Please be first."

At that moment the door to the inner office opened and the secretary invited either of the applicants to come in for a job interview. Linda exchanged a quick glance with her sister and received the necessary encouragement to be first. With dignity and poise, but with her heart pounding a fast, unsteady rhythm, she entered, then sat on the sofa by the desk. She listened intently to the requirements, the expectations, the opportunities, and the benefits of the job.

With confidence reinforced and strengthened through Mary's encouraging whispers, Linda related her experiences and preparation that would be of particular value in the work the employer had just outlined. Her excitement at the possibility of employment was evident and continued to increase. With this part-time job on campus she would be able to continue her education, pay back her loan, and live in the dormitory with her friends and her sister. It all seemed too good to be true, and yet there was a possibility.

With a prayer in her heart, she waited. The interview apparently completed, the employer glanced out the window thoughtfully.

Then, turning to face Linda, she asked, "And if I hire you for the job, what about your sister?"

Like air rapidly escaping from an inflated balloon, Linda's enthusiasm quickly slipped away. There was only one job opening! Somehow the advertisement in the university paper had given her the impression that there were many. Now she was in competition with her sister for the same job.

With great effort, she managed to hide her disappointment and regain some of her original enthusiasm. In that moment, her personal interests were set aside. With both hands outstretched to provide additional emphasis, she took up the cause for her sister. "If there is only one opening, just one job, please talk to my sister, Mary." Then she rose to leave. In one last attempt to speak for her sister, she explained, "My sister worked long, long hours while I was on my mission. She saved every penny she could so that when I returned we could both come to school. I know she sacrificed a lot just for me, just so we could be together. My little sister did that all for me." Her voice softened, and tears filled her eyes. "I wouldn't even be here if it weren't for Mary. When you meet her, you'll know what I mean."

Linda regained her composure and returned to the outer office, where Mary was waiting. She whispered, "Good luck!" and they exchanged places. Inside the employer's office the same procedures were covered and the same details presented. Mary's enthusiasm was equal to that of Linda—a fresh, unsophisticated, honest eagerness to obtain part-time employment.

Mary, sensitive to the reality of the situation, was anxious to inquire about Linda before pushing further in her own behalf. "What about my sister?" she asked. Somewhat hesitatingly, the employer confirmed what Mary had feared. "There is only one job opening at this time," was the response.

Like a faithful evangelist, Mary took up her sister's cause. "My sister is the one you want," she said. "She's a returned missionary and has the ability to meet people much better than I. Everyone loves Linda. If there is only one opening, please consider Linda."

The deep feelings of love, concern, and loyalty these young women expressed for each other interested the employer more than the immediate task of filling a job. Neither knew of the other's advocacy.

At the conclusion of the interview the employer asked Mary to remain seated, then stepped to the door and invited Linda in. The sisters sat side by side, obviously renewed by the strength of being together. The formality of the interviews had been replaced now by a spirit of expectation as each wanted most what she thought was best for the other. They listened intently while the employer carefully, and with obvious emotion, unfolded the moving details of the past hour.

When Mary heard the details of Linda's interview, her head dropped. She reached over to clasp Linda's hand, and they glanced at each other. Tears filled their eyes as Mary leaned close to Linda and murmured, "But it's no more than you would have done for me, if I'd been called on a mission."

The employer then related the details of Mary's interview while Linda learned how her sister had set aside her own personal desires. Linda's feelings of love and appreciation now demanded even further expression. "Mary has more love in her heart than anyone I've ever met. She has an unselfish quality of giving and being able to serve others so willingly. It's the spirit of Christ, and she's got it more than I have. That's what I'm striving to develop."

Mary interrupted her sister. "But you gave yourself totally on your mission. Let me tell you, you did!" Then, turning to the employer, she spoke with deep emotion. "You see, Linda is three years older than I am and she has paved the way for me through all the difficult times when I was younger. I haven't reached her height yet, but she stands by me all the way."

Linda, smiling through her tears, responded, "She's my sister. I always will."

# Tithing in Full

"Is the bishop there?" The voice on the other end of the line was breathless and anxious when I answered the phone on the first ring.

Since her tone indicated such urgency, I hesitated to explain that the bishop wasn't in just then, but she quickly interrupted my explanation. "How long before he'll be there?" she asked.

I found myself speaking rapidly as I too caught her excitement. I quickly explained that he had been called to a neighbor's home for a few minutes and should be right back. "Good," she said. "I'll come and wait."

I didn't recognize the voice, and before I could say another word, I heard the click of the receiver in my ear.

It was a beautiful May afternoon. All day I could hear the shrill voices of youth mingled occasionally with the rhythmic beating of the drums of the marching band at the high school just a few blocks away. The happy sounds had kept me moving through my house-work at a steady pace. I carefully put the final touches on the living room carpet, making sure the nap all went the same way. Then, standing in the doorway to avoid leaving footprints in the carpet, I admired the sprig of apricot blossoms I had placed on the mantel.

Just then the doorbell rang. Before I could answer it, Julie, a senior at the high school, came bounding into the living room and made a direct landing on the green and white loveseat near the window. I followed right behind her with no concern for the footprints in the carpet.

She was talking excitedly as she came in, and said something about having run five blocks up the hill. She was so out of breath it was impossible to make sense of what she was trying to say. She was clutching a handful of dollar bills. Then she emptied the contents of her little bag, and one-dollar bills fell out everywhere, some blending into the green carpet as they landed on the floor.

Still excitedly bouncing up and down, she asked again, "When will the bishop be back?" Then, without waiting for an answer, she said, "Oh, I'll tell you," and she began her story in detail. Just before she finished, the bishop returned and quietly took a seat. Without pausing, Julie began again from the beginning to relate her story, but this time her excitement seemed a bit more subdued.

She explained how she had been working three jobs while going to school, in hopes of raising enough money to go to college in the fall. Because of many unexpected expenses, though, she had somehow slipped behind on her tithing. This had given her considerable concern, because she knew the importance of tithing and somehow had to make it up.

As she shifted to a different position, she told about the most exciting thing that had happened at school that day. Every member of the senior class had secretly hoped they would be selected to receive either a fifty-dollar cash award or an old car that the entire student body had been admiring. Julie explained how the very thought of fifty dollars struck a responsive chord with her, since that was the exact amount required to bring her tithing up to date. She told of having a strong feeling to say a silent prayer and to promise that if she should receive the award, she would take the money and give it to the bishop for tithing just as soon as she could.

At this point Julie's voice took on a more serious tone. Her name had been announced, and she was called up to receive the award. Then the struggle began. Immediately all of her friends gathered around to share her excitement and give counsel. Of course she should take the car, they seemed to agree. One of the boys who really mattered to her said, "You've got to take the car. You can sell it for more than fifty dollars." A chorus of friends joined in, telling her that the only right thing to do was to take the car.

It was that statement, "the only right thing to do," that set her course. For Julie, there was only one right thing to do. She had already made a promise of which her friends were not aware. She must get to the bishop with the fifty dollars.

Leaving her friends somewhat bewildered, she ran to the telephone in the school office and called the information operator for the number—that would be quicker than trying to find the name in the directory.

She paused now for the first time during the full accounting, as if to say, "And here I am." Then she took a deep breath, looked directly at the bishop, and, with eyes brimming over with tears, declared, "Here's my tithing in full."

I glanced from Julie to the bishop. With a warm, sensitive expression and tears filling his eyes, he reached for Julie's hand. Quietly I left the room, to allow for that private moment when one stands alone to give an accounting to and receive acceptance from one appointed by the power of heaven.

Half an hour passed, and I joined them again at the door as Julie was ready to leave. She was smiling now, her tear-stained face radiating an expression of victory, like one having conquered self.

"Thank you, thank you so much, bishop," she said, and the bishop replied, "I thank *you,* Julie, and your Father in heaven thanks you too."

She was half running, half skipping, by the time she reached the end of our sidewalk and turned north. The bishop and I stood in the doorway watching her. Just before she got out of sight, she turned and waved, then went on her happy way.

The bishop quietly closed the door, meditating aloud as he said, "The Lord's way is always a happy way."

# Index